YOUR THIRD ACT

A GUIDE TO A
GREAT RETIREMENT

By

William S. Cook, Jr., M.D.

Grant D. Fairley

Published By:

Silverwoods Publishing - a division of McK Consulting Inc.

Toronto ~ Chicago

www.silverwoods-publishing.com

ISBN 978-1-897202-34-0

Cover Design by Artist's Tree
Cover Photo – rgbspace/bigstock.com

Printed in the United States of America

First Edition

DEDICATION

This book is dedicated to all those
who choose to embrace the changes, challenges,
and opportunities of their retirement adventure.

AUTHORS' NOTE

"And what about very old friends?" Gandalf asked at Bilbo's door.

Bill Cook and Grant Fairley met in 1977 at Wheaton College in Wheaton, Illinois, where Bill was a senior from the Deep South and Grant was a freshman from Canada. Like many schools, Wheaton paired older students with new ones to help them integrate into college life and to share the perspectives of someone further down the road. These relationships were helpful for many incoming students and made a great orientation program.

In the case of the two authors, the friendship that began there has continued to this day. While they shared a liberal arts education at the storied school, their careers were destined to go in very different directions. Life eventually took Bill back to Mississippi while Grant returned to Ontario.

It is a delight that these very different life journeys can now merge once again in the creation of this book almost forty years later.

Old friends indeed.

TABLE OF CONTENTS

IN APPRECIATION

Special thanks goes to Barbara Beibers, who transcribed Dr. Cook's dictation. Jeny Lyn Ruelo once again did great work in laying out the book. The cover design was by Cari Fairley with generous advice from graphic artist, Sam Beibers. Paul Archie Teleron was very helpful in handling our digital images. Editing by Megan Van Dyke improved the clarity of the book. We are grateful for the photography of Dr. Cook by Kim Preston and Grant Fairley's cover photograph was taken by Matthew Page.

INTRODUCTION

As more people cross over the retirement line each day, each one faces the question, "What's next?"

Some find it hard to believe that a career or series of careers is now officially done with the passing of a particular birthday, years of service, or reaching their magic number. Many people spend much of their working lives wondering if they will ever make it. Others see the arrival of the "gold watch" as a sign of achievement leading to a long awaited liberation from the routines of life. Some have been retired not by choice but by down-sizing, right-sizing, outsourcing, technology, a bad economy, creative destruction, innovation, or other strangely named market forces.

Most people find entering retirement to be a mix of emotions. There can be satisfaction for a job well done. An excitement comes with new freedoms and flexibility. It is not unusual to also experience some fear and uncertainty. You face questions of aging as you assume the title of retiree. Financial changes can be stressful as you start to live off a pension and whatever retirement plan you cobbled together during your working years. Another challenge is more subtle and more important – what is your purpose in the next chapters of your life?

In this book, we will explore with you some of the big ideas baby boomers must consider as they face a coming retirement or have already crossed that career finish line. At the heart of the book, you will find commitment to finishing strong and well.

The purpose of this book is to give a broad overview of a number of topics relevant to those approaching retirement, those who have retired, and some who will never retire!

You will find in this book, discussions on topics relating to health, finances, legal matters, careers, relationships and more. This book is not a substitute for receiving the appropriate professional advice that is specific to you and your needs.

Always consult your healthcare professionals, legal advisors, financial advisors, and others to discover what decisions are best for you considering your unique circumstances.

At one of our meetings for the book, Grant asked Bill, as a geriatric psychiatrist, at what age someone is considered a "geriatric." When Bill responded that the age is 55, Grant, who was then 56, slumped forward. He realized that this was now a self-help book.

Welcome to the next adventure!

THE THIRD ACT

For those who love the theater, there is a sweet sorrow associated with the third act of the play. The intermission usually warns that more than half the experience is over. When the curtain rises on the third act, you know that the journey with the characters and story of the play will soon be done.

The first act is a time of introduction. We meet the main characters. We explore the time and setting of the play. The costumes and speech give us a context for what will develop. Before long, we find out whether this is the best of times or the worst of times for our protagonist. In some plays, it is just another day. There are often hints of what might follow. Conflict. Mystery. Passion. Suspense. The themes begin to show.

In a play that is well written, the words begin to enchant us. If the performances are good, we start to share the journey with the characters. The distance between the audience and the stage disappears. The theater becomes one. It does not seem like very long before the first act is over.

In the second act, the story takes on a more defined shape. Energy grows. What was begun now has momentum. Problems intensify. Opportunities are richer. The plot may twist and turn. Danger and risk can abound. Will it be triumph or despair? With a good play, we now are invested in the story and the future of the characters. In most performances, we begin that ride to the top as the story and the action intensifies. It reaches its climax late in the second act. We hold our breath. The intermission arrives to let us breathe again.

Resuming our seats, we have some important expectations for the third act. We do not expect it to be the time when the action is at its height. That is over. What we need and often demand from the third act is to help us make sense of what we just experienced.

Awaiting the audience is the rest of the story. How will the characters deal with the victory or defeat? Losses are to be mourned. The successes are to be celebrated. Whether or not the story ends on a happy or sad note does not matter as much as that it ends well. How will the story teller wrap it up for us?

We want resolution where possible. It is hoped that the playwright will reveal the last of the mysteries and answer the lingering questions. It is the act where the battlefield is replaced by the journey home.

What is the test of a great third act? Satisfaction. That doesn't necessarily mean happiness or sadness. Often, it is a combination of success and the price paid. The hero may live but be forever scarred. Whatever the heroine endured, she is stronger, wiser, or richer for the experience. Always, they are changed from the persons we met in the first act.

End a story well, and you have a satisfied audience. Fail to satisfy them, and a great story is lost.

How often have you left a play, movie, or book with the sense of, "This is all wrong"? "That was a terrible ending" will change the recommendation of that performance. The audience can feel betrayed or cheated when the writer treats the third act merely as something to hurry through now that the climax of the story is complete.

If you spent some time reviewing your life's story as a play, how would you describe the first two acts? Like most people, you too will have your cast of characters who journey along the road with you for longer or shorter periods. Some of the early themes that are present as your life takes the inevitable twists unalterably mark our second acts. Who would play the parts if your life story was a movie or a play? What would the genre be for your story? Mystery? Drama? Comedy? Romance? War? Adventure?

Perhaps you can point to the peak in the tale. It might be reaching the top of your profession. Was it overcoming what seemed like an impossible obstacle? Maybe it was fulfilling your role as a spouse and parent as you saw your children grow from dependence to independence and finally to that sometimes elusive interdependence. On some level, the hopes and dreams of that first act are realized or changed by what life became. Our choices for better and worse, along with those of the others in our story, combine with the larger fabric of life to reach the climax of our play.

For people who pay attention to their stories, they can tell you exactly where they are in their tale no matter where they are along the road in their first and second acts. The ups and downs can be charted and described along with the feelings of happiness, frustration, sadness, and joy they have known along the way. The characters in their story can be identified, including the part each played in the telling of our life's journey. Still, they know that how this all will make sense has yet to be determined. That's saved for the third act.

Depending on where you are in your story, the intermission curtain may not have come down yet. You may notice it coming down now, or you might be able to look back and see when the intermission began. At some point, you find yourself in the third act.

If we live long enough, the third act gives us an opportunity to begin to make sense of our story. Taking time to reflect on the experiences we have added through the pages and chapters of life can give us a renewed sense of meaning.

Significantly, it is in the third act that most of us begin to fully appreciate the other characters in our story. With the distance traveled since our first act, we now start to understand the role that our parents, grandparents, and other family members played for us. The teachers, coaches, and early friendships now can be seen for the important contributions that they made to us. The high school and college years that defined our part of the generation continue to echo in our preferences and tastes. Early experiences that brought us joy or pain become threads that we can often trace throughout our lives.

Successes and failures in relationships begin to sort themselves out. With new honesty, we can appreciate the ways we helped and hurt those we loved. Reflecting on how our family took shape, seeing the arc of each one facing the challenges of early life, reaching adulthood and beyond, all begin to bring us clarity. Some of the best of friends left our stories. Unexpected people entered our tales and became new friends for life.

The career we began may have included many jobs that were quite different from what we expected. The dreams of the future we envisioned in our college years gave way to what became our story. Times that seemed wasted may now connect with opportunities that were waiting, if unseen, at the time. Interests begun by whim or chance may have stayed with us throughout life.

You may be a person who has a faith perspective that includes a sense of providence along the way. The third act may be the place where you begin to see how all these pieces of your puzzle start to fit together. Stepping back, you see the many threads actually form a design that, for all its shades and hues, is distinctly yours. The feeling of having been part of a larger purpose can bring you to a sense of peace with your experiences, for good or for ill.

You may or may not be in the third act yet. When you get there, take the time to make it count. What can you do with your third act?

You will not be able to undo all the mistakes of the past. All the missed opportunities will not reappear. Some of those who were there to support and encourage you will be gone. Time is no longer on your side.

But, while you live and breathe, you are still on stage. Look around at the relationships in your life. What can you choose to do to improve the lives of others? How can you help those in need? What can you do to mentor those who are still in the most challenging time of life? Encouragement is always in short supply in our world. Where can you encourage others?

Living a life that seeks to benefit others is a worthy calling at any time in life. It can be especially rewarding for those in the third act. The importance of ambitions and the grasping of younger years now fade next to the desire for strong relationships and purpose. Who we have in our life becomes more important than what we have.

How will you be remembered? The promise of your youth and the triumphs and defeats of your life may be recalled or forgotten. For those who know you, the third act will leave a lasting impression. It may enhance a good or great life. It may redeem a life of disappointment or failure. At its best, the third act offers the possibility of satisfaction for you and those in your story. The final curtain is never far away. Use the scenes you have left to finish well.

PARTY ON!

Retirement parties are meant to be a time of celebration, although often they are dreaded both by the retiree and the ones arranging the farewell. What makes for a great retirement party?

It begins with knowing how the retiree feels about their retirement. The retiree may have strong feelings about this stately occasion that marks the end of a career. They may take it in stride as just another day on the calendar.

For those who have been counting the years, then the months, and finally the days, it is a great relief. Part of this could be the anticipated freedom that is expected in the retirement years. Others may have felt their work becoming more and more difficult to do as age or changing workplaces make each day more challenging. Many see it as a major accomplishment to have seen the conclusion of the work done over twenty or thirty years of service. They may recognize that many of those who started with them never made it to retirement due to health challenges, death, layoffs, or forced retirements.

Some retirees face retirement with a great dread. This event usually triggers a financial change as you move from your regular earnings to life on a pension or retirement savings supplemented by whatever government contribution follows. Benefits may also be reduced or lost before the retiree is eligible for some of the government programs. That can lead to worry and stress.

Many people find their self-image closely tied to their work. In response to the question, "Who am I?" they answer, "I work at..." or "My profession is..." To suddenly have to begin the answer as, "I used to work at..." or "I am a retired..." may change the way people think of themselves. They also worry how others will view them. Some think to be retired is to be irrelevant. "I am not indispensable, they have moved on without me. People will treat me differently."

A classic example of this was the character of Major General Waverly in the movie White Christmas. After commanding a division during World War II, he retires. His retirement plan is to have a country inn in Vermont. The movie shows the restlessness of a man who was used to making consequential decisions with great responsibilities. He even tried to return to active duty. As Bing Crosby's character reads the response from the military, the general is crushed as he recognizes that his is no longer needed. One of the Irving Berlin songs in the movie was, "What Can You Do with a General?", which questions the value of life in retirement.

Another fear of retirement is related to the loss of relationships. Most work environments include a number of people with whom you work over a period of time. Some may be friends while others are just colleagues. All those social interactions do fill up some of the human need for social relationships. To suddenly remove five, ten, or fifty daily relationships from your life is to make a great change in your social network. That even includes the colleagues who have driven you crazy over the years. The prospect of being home all the time may not be the retiree's idea of a great time – and many spouses who find their routines changed by this would agree.

Depending on the social network of the previous retirees of the organization, they may already have established a club or association that regularly gathers the past employees for a time together. This allows the connections with their past working life and colleagues to continue in support of one another. This is a wise move for organizations to initiate and facilitate where possible. Including retirees on the list of company newsletters and communications would also be a positive move. Like anything, some retirees will value the opportunities while others will not.

For the retirees who have waited in great anticipation of that magic retirement date, the end of the job is the beginning of their freedom to do what they want to do.

Increasingly, retirement from a job is only a pause in the career. Following retirement, many begin work as consultants – sometimes for the very organizations they left. Others take a new full-time role somewhere else or perhaps reduce their commitments and start a part-time job.

For extroverts, the idea of a party is business at its best. For those who are introverts, they may find the whole idea of being the focus of such an event painful, even if a number of people are being celebrated at the same time. This is an important time for others to be able to recognize your part in their story. So, while the temptation is to ask them to mail you the gold watch or leave a piece of cake on your desk, it is one of those august occasions that require your presence. It will hopefully be something you can remember fondly, even if it is difficult at the time.

To have a great retirement party, the retiree needs to prepare mentally and emotionally for the event. You may be invited to express what kind of party you prefer, or it may be a standard format that the organization always uses. Be prepared with your preferences if asked. It is not helpful for those planning the event for you to be too coy or humble at this point. If they ask for input, be ready to share some ideas. Of course, you want to avoid the tendency some people have to pull out a full list of detailed expectations, essentially having planned the party for them.

For those who want to have the best chance of having a great and meaningful retirement party when their time comes, you should join the committee now to help in the planning of other retirement celebrations. Organizations with a tradition of doing retirements well are remembered differently than those who check the calendar and realize they have to have "another one of those things" again.

For those planning the party, identify what budget you have been given, if any. If no traditional gift or recognition is established, you may want to give people the opportunity to contribute to a gift. If the retiree's spouse or family can be contacted, ask what kind of gift ideas would be meaningful. Discover any other preferences that might be helpful in planning, particularly if there is only one retiree being celebrated. Find out how many invitations should be available for family and friends to receive for the event if it is after work. Always try to include the retiree's spouse and children if possible, since that will add to the memory of the occasion and provide support for those retirees who find those social times stressful.

Speeches can make or break any social event. Plan to have one person do the recognition of the retiree. That may be a close colleague or the leader of the organization. Those giving the speech should take the time to talk to the worker's colleagues. Ask a simple question: "What word or phrase best describes the retiree?" You often find relational strengths that colleagues have appreciated that may not be part of the job itself. Those traits of kindness, a great sense of humor, or being likeable trump diligence, efficiency, and a great focus on the task at times like this. The speaker should of course identify any special contributions the person has made to the organization over their career in addition to the basic facts of their service, for instance, how long they have served and what positions they held. Usually a speech of 5-10 minutes is much more welcome than an oration that leaves the audience restless and planning their escape. If there are multiple speakers, an emcee that will tactfully enforce time limits is essential.

An opportunity for one of the family to say a few words can be positive if the family member is prepared and comfortable speaking.

It is always a good idea to give the retiree an opportunity to respond to the speech(es) with a thank-you or a few words of reflection. Retirees who have paid attention during other people's parties will also recognize the value of a short response vs. a long speech.

The most valuable part of the event is the opportunity for colleagues and friends to have the time to visit with the retiree. It is a bonus if you can have this time before the formal part of the program where everyone is gathered. That sets the tone for the actual event. Then, after the speeches and presentation, encourage people to stay and visit. In addition to being positive for the retiree, this also creates bonds with the employees who are continuing. One of the most common mistakes in retirement parties is to have a venue where the music is too loud or the configuration of the tables does not allow people to mingle with the retirees.

Great retirement parties celebrate the person, not the employee. Their contributions to the organization are included, but if that is the only expression at the event, it is easy to see that they were only valued for what they did. Value the retiree as a person in the planning and activities of the event, and it will be a celebration that everyone will enjoy and remember.

The closing scene of White Christmas with the general surrounded by men who traveled there to honor him was the retirement party he never had. The efforts of Wallace and Davis et al. to give their best to a man who had served them well enriched all who were there. The story, songs, and the long-awaited snow made it a movie the world loves to enjoy.

CLIMBING THE TREE

The tendency to look back on our lives begins as we enter new decades where our routines are so different from the earlier years of play, school, and the many firsts of our twenties. Our hindsight does not need to be remarkable since none of that was very long ago.

As the decades roll on, the memories of the sights, sounds, people, and places of our past become a bit harder to reconstruct. We also tend to start using a softer lens as we recreate those memories of what every generation calls, "The Good Old Days."

For many people, the passing of earlier generations triggers a desire to look even further back in time. We begin to seek our family tree. It often begins with a discovery about a grandparent or parent that reveals something different from what we have known. Many of those from earlier generations were not inclined to talk about their past. Lost loves, wars waged, and an economic depression survived simply made up life as it was. Everyone experienced it, so why talk about it? They also were forward-looking generations, hopeful for the offspring who would follow to have a better tomorrow than their today.

If you find that one piece of history or have a nagging question about an ancestor, you may be in danger of catching the family tree bug. This is particularly true if you find some answers to your questions. Before you know it, you understand that many bits and pieces from the past can be discovered. The World Wide Web with its myriad bits of information combined with government and newspaper records allows you to become a family tree detective. Many ancestry services enable you to start assembling the stories of those who went before.

Depending on your country(s) of origin, you may be able to go back a long way in discovering the meaning of the Biblical term "begat" as you see a list growing of children and parents. As names, birth years, baptisms, marriages, deaths, and more are gathered, some of the milestones of your ancestry begin to emerge. Some entries remain as names only. Others have additional facts to add. When very successful, you might have pictures, newspaper accounts, letters, or books that talk about members of your family tree.

Often, there are members of a family who enjoy this type of hunt. Other siblings or cousins may value the results but not find the process to be of any interest. There seems to be no rhyme or reason as to which family members might take up the quest. If you are fortunate enough to come from a family where one or more of the members in previous generations kept records, you are way ahead. Not long ago, many families would have family trees, with whatever data, all created by hand. Often it was the family Bible that included the generational record. Some families faithfully noted the additions and passings within the family so that their family tree would be up to date.

Now, in our fifties and sixties, we realize the many questions we wish we had asked of the family members we knew then but who are now gone. Like many facets of life, we learn too late what we should have known and what we might later want to know.

For those who can explore their family roots, many discover that some of the family traits seen in their family tree have also appeared in the later generations. Some say that we are more like our grandparents. As you discover their stories or interests, you might begin to see echoes of them in your life as well. Some of those echoes might be physical characteristics. That is not so surprising. Many also find that it extends to personality, temperament, and even idiosyncrasies of those earlier relatives.

If you are one of those who finds themselves climbing the family tree, be prepared to discover the simple lives lived well, the adventurers who lived large, and others who had shining moments. Like all generations, some will have had a steady response to life. Others may have had huge successes or dismal failures. You will find some who qualify as "characters"

– with all that means. Some of the best relatives may have little recorded about them as they spent their lives toiling to raise and support their family. You soon find that all their lives had value, and much depended on when they lived and where they lived. They all learned the joys of living along with the sorrows that the journey brings. That can be a comfort and an encouragement for us as we carry on the family story.

If you are one of those from your generation who has the bug, you have the opportunity to help recreate the stories of those of your family who otherwise sit silently on the branches above in your family tree. The discovery and the storytelling will enrich the current generation and those who will follow.

MAPLE SYRUP

As the countdown to retirement begins, we start to imagine a new life. One of the big changes we visualize is freedom from the clock. While the baby boomer generation has identified age as an enemy, we would contend that it is actually a friend. It is not a perfect friend, of course, but a valuable companion that journeys with us. Like the best of old friends, age knew us back when we were young and has continued with us all these years. As you come to understand the aging process, you will learn that there are gifts given to us even as we experience the losses that are also part of the passing of time.

One of the advantages of getting older is that you begin to be able to step back outside of your present timeline and see it as part of a larger journey. That perspective is part of taking our knowledge and seeing it transform into something more valuable – wisdom.

Occasionally, you might meet a younger person who could be considered "wise beyond their years." But, in most cases, wisdom comes along with both time and experience. The other essentials are the willingness and effort to reflect on what you have learned and experienced. Reflection is more and more difficult to do as we live in an instant society that values now more than then. A wise person understands that we need a balance between then, now, and next. All contribute to a balanced life and a productive future.

In our early years, we accumulate a vast amount of knowledge very quickly. If you have observed the sheer volume of complex information that infants and toddlers absorb and process in their earliest years, you have to marvel at the pliable human brain. Throughout our years of schooling, we continue to accumulate more and more information to help us prepare for life and work. Add to that all of the social information that we gather through our family, friendships, and other relationships. Human beings certainly are knowledgeable.

For those who live or who have visited the northern forests around the Great Lakes over to Vermont and Quebec, you learn that one of the favorite forms of agriculture there is not enacted on the ground or on trees. It is done within trees. Unlike most crops, it is harvested when the ground is often still covered in snow. That late winter-early spring delight is maple syrup. There is nothing like enjoying pancakes or waffles topped with real maple syrup.

The traditional process of making maple syrup includes using metal taps or spigots that are hammered into the trees when the sap is running. That is usually at the end of winter as spring is battling for supremacy. The cool nights and warmer days allow the sap to run. From these taps come the drips of the sugar maple's sap into the buckets. As the buckets fill, they are taken to the sugar shack to go through a number of stages of boiling. At each stage, the sap becomes more and more concentrated as the water in the liquid evaporates. It is a slow and time-consuming process (more modern maple syrup farms use bore holes and tubes that run into the processing building). The ratio of sap to syrup from a sugar maple is about 40:1. That means you would need to boil 10 gallons of sap to get one quart of syrup.

Transforming our knowledge and experience into wisdom is a similar process. Through reflection, we have to process the volume of information we know and have experienced to approach what we call wisdom. Like the fires of the sugar shack, it is often our difficult challenges that bring us to know the benefits of a wise life.

As the process of time and aging seems to take away many of our abilities and relationships, we do gain a perspective on life that allows us to deal with new challenges in a more positive way. Wisdom teaches us that as we have survived so many difficulties in the normal course of life, these new challenges will be managed as well.

That kind of serenity and worldview makes the later years of life some of the most rewarding. The journey we began so many years ago that was full of unknowns and uncertainties now gives way to a quiet confidence that we can meet any problems as they come along.

This quality also makes us very valuable in our family and community groups. While avoiding the clichéd, "In my day…", we can still use our stories to draw comparisons to present problems so that people will see beyond the immediate crisis. From our experiences, we can "en-courage" or "lend courage" to those in our lives in the same way battle-hardened soldiers can give courage to new troops who are understandably afraid of the unknowns they will face.

One of the great fears of entering retirement and beyond is that we will no longer be relevant or needed in our family or society. We may find it more difficult to keep up with all the rapidly advancing technology and information in our changing world once we leave the workplace. Do commit to being a life-long learner – that's an important investment in your brain health and social well-being. What we can bring to any table is the wisdom that no amount of knowledge by itself can match.

Wisdom allows us and those we mentor to take a wider view and to avoid the risks of being governed by our many impulses like fear and greed. While acknowledging the emotions that others are facing, we add stories that give others the confidence that they too will overcome their challenges and that they will survive these tests.

When you earn that role in your family or other circles of your life, you find that the trials of fire that were part of your story now leave a sweeter taste of satisfaction as you help those in your life.

BON VOYAGE

Those living in North America are blessed with many wonderful places to visit. From the stunning vistas of the Rockies to the deep calm of the arctic to the warmth of California, you can spend a lifetime experiencing it all and never come close to knowing it. Waters like the Great Lakes or the mighty Mississippi River in the heartland contrast with the coasts of New England and the Maritime Provinces so different again from the Gulf Coast. The never ending prairies, the deep forests of British Columbia, the deserts of the south west and the rolling meadows of Kentucky all are part of this diverse continent.

Many baby boomers grew up with the annual summer vacation trip where they would visit classic tourist destinations like national parks, big cities, or beaches. The interstate highways created during the Eisenhower years and the expansion of the Trans-Canada highway and the 400 series in Ontario meant that you could gather the family into the then large cars and head off on an adventure. We grew up in the age when campsites, motels, and hotels had just appeared to offer a break from the great distances between destinations on the continent. Family photo albums, slide carousels, and primitive movies recall those trips and those days. Increased vacations and a stronger middle-class meant travel was no longer for the wealthy alone.

As the boomers became teens and entered their twenties, hitching a ride or taking that old muscle car or rust bucket on cheap gas meant you could create your own memories too. Some enjoyed a gap year and back-packed through the hostels of Europe. Educational or service trips also expanded the horizons of the boomer generation.

The boomers also benefited from the earlier trends of summer camps that began in the 1930s. Around the same time, the idea of a family cottage or cabin meant that some families would return to the familiar place for their summer break rather than traveling great distances.

By the time the boomers became adults with children of their own, most families had both parents working, and we were beginning to see inflation cut into budgets for these summer rituals. Still, many families found a way to hit the road to visit somewhere new or special. New memories were made with Polaroid instant cameras and Super-8 movies. Children of the boomers were encouraged to have a taste of the experiences that the boomers had treasured from their earliest years. The family rituals would continue even as they were updated.

While some had the opportunity to travel extensively throughout their lives, many find that the desire to travel intensifies as your children leave home. Deferred due to mortgages and college funds, boomers turn to travel as one of the important leisure pursuits before and during retirement.

Travel now is no longer limited to where we can go on a tank or two of gas. Opportunities to fly to other countries to explore different cultures and scenery allow us to step into the exotic or historic places a world away. Travel and adventure on cruises, tours, and eco-trips and the intrepid souls who venture off with nothing in particular planned all contribute to a huge industry.

Why do we travel?

Visiting a destination on a long-delayed trip brings a strong sense of satisfaction when it is finally possible. It is stimulating to visit places that are not home. That quality of "other" that defines travel and vacations can be as different for each of us as we all are. Travel is also a reward at a time later in life when obligations give way to opportunities. It is also used to mark major events like retirement or a significant birthday or anniversary.

We have traded the crowded family station wagon of our youth for the crowded airports, security lines, delayed flights, and tight airplane rows of our later years. Somehow it is fitting.

The difference for the travelling boomers is that the ritual question, "Are we there yet?" is no longer asked by us to our parents or by our children to us. In the sense of our life journey, we can now answer, "We have arrived!"

EXPLORING THE PASTURE

Unwanted retirement can be a very difficult experience.

You may face it because a date on the calendar announces you have reached an age that suggests what you could have done successfully yesterday, you can no longer do tomorrow. The "factor," that mathematical term from your school days, may now force a calculation of your age and years of service that results in you receiving congratulations on your retirement. Companies that are downsizing or restructuring might make you an offer you wish to take or perhaps may not refuse. More senior people who include a higher price tag of wages and benefits are prime targets for companies that want to be more lean and mean. New demands for training, skills, and flexibility more easily found in the young may entice a government or company to transition their older workforce into the category of their pensioned former employees.

However you arrived there, if retirement was not the much-anticipated day of liberation in your plans, you may find yourself facing fears and disappointment that you now have the label "retired" associated with your name.

You were not ready to be put out to pasture. What do you do next?

Much of how you will fare in retirement will depend on your mindset. If you spend your energy fighting your new reality with every fiber of your being, expect a blend of frustration and despair to be the new normal for your days.

Anything in life that involves loss does trigger a grieving process. The loss of employment is not just a loss of income but also of relationships and elements of your identity. This is especially true if you consider what you do to be a major part of who you are. A forced retirement can impose a loss of control over your life in a big way. While on some level we all understand that any job is temporary, the day-to-day work over a period of years dulls our senses and lulls us into the belief that everything will continue much as it always had.

Recognize the loss. Accept the feelings. Decide to move on. Each of those decisions are made in stages, not moments. They are decisions that will need to be reaffirmed on days when it seems very difficult to move forward. But gradually, you will find the strength to move beyond the sense of doom that a forced retirement might cause you to feel.

As part of moving forward, it is a good idea to embrace your new place. If they have put you out to pasture – explore the pasture.

In it, you may find not only new things to do, new people to engage, and new interests to follow – you may also find out more about yourself.

In the grind that we call everyday, it is possible for us to become shaped and molded into what we do. Our identity and our work become one, ignoring the many dimensions of what it means to be human and what it means to be you. The change that retirement brings can uncover new possibilities in the world around you.

Perhaps there is a new or different work opportunity there. Talents and interests undeveloped due to the lack of time and energy may now be something you can begin to explore. Some people pursue knowledge of subjects that were unrelated to work and therefore deferred all these years. Travel to familiar places or new ones may await.

Exploring the pasture is mostly about exploring yourself. Who are you? What do you care about? What would you like to do? Who would you like to be with? How will you spend your time?

So, if your story now includes the word retired, do not despair. Open your eyes, your mind, and your heart. You might find some pleasant surprises waiting for you in the new pasture.

CREATING YOUR BUSINESS CARD

For those who see retirement as just a pause until their next position in the workplace, one of the important concepts to address is, "What does your business card say?"

In this case, we do not mean your literal business card. Think of the role that a business card plays in the workplace. It is your introduction before or at a meeting. It also may be something you leave at the end of your meeting. In all cases, it announces who you are, what you do, and how you may be reached.

You might be someone who is going to leave your current employment and return to your company or industry as a contractor or consultant. There, you will continue to be recognized by those in your sphere who knew of you from before. However, do not be surprised if you are treated differently even by those former members of your team. There are changes in how you are perceived once your have a different role because you have already retired.

If you are reaching out to others in your industry or trying something new, it is helpful to prepare to explain what your business card announces. Could you provide a couple of paragraphs for each of the points on a typical business card? You will need to know that and more to move forward into your new venture.

The first question is, "Who are you?" Your name is a good start but hardly enough. You might attach your previous employment to your name. Do you include retired? Go beyond that surface information. Who are you really? What motivates you? What do you value? Why does work matter to you? What do you hope for your future? These and many more questions start to define who you are. If you have been in your pre-retirement position for a long time, you may not have gone through that type of exercise for many years. Take the time to reflect on yourself as a person.

"What do you do?" is the second question a business card answers. Some of this is clear from your title. Accountant. Nurse. Elementary Teacher. Police Officer. Many titles are by definition (and often intentionally) vague. Consultant. Administrator. Executive. Advisor. Coordinator. The flexibility that the title includes may suggest that you can morph into a variety of roles. It may also suggest, "Tell me what you need done and I'll see if I can do it!" Looking back over your career, what are the things that you did well? Where were your talents recognized by others? What qualities did you bring to your role to make others successful? These are the beginnings of identifying what you would be suited and willing to do in the future.

Answering the question of how you may be reached requires more than just a phone number or email address. In defining your life's work after retirement, recognize the importance of how you connect with other people. As we continue in a long-term job, it is easy for us to continue relating to people as we did in our old role. Relating to people outside of your established relationships is different. Over time, people learn how to communicate with us and us with them. You know what type of communication works well with different people, and you avoid using methods that create conflict.

Moving to a new role – especially if you are going to have to sell your experience and qualifications to others – means that you might need to brush up on your communication skills. Otherwise, you will miss opportunities because you will not effectively reach those on the other end of the conversation.

There are many useful resources that can help you brush up on your interpersonal communication skills. One tool that is both intuitive and useful is psycho-geometrics, developed by Dr. Susan Dellinger. This will help you recognize not only your own but others' communication styles.

It will help you read other people and reach out to them in ways that they will understand and appreciate. If you have never explored this, it is a great place to start.

It is also helpful for those of you venturing back into the working world to spend some time with an individual or team that can assist you in writing a new resume or review your business plan to give you some feedback on your objectives. Executive or career coaches can also help you sharpen your skills and add new tools to your toolbox. All of this is important preparation before you venture out into the world beyond your old job. It is not only career development; it will help your personal development as well.

Then, the small piece of paper you pass along to a contact will mean so much more than the words and numbers that appear on its face. It will be a short summary of the great opportunity that is standing in front of them.

AROUND YOUR CAMPFIRE

Many of us grew up with the joys of a campfire. Like a living being, the campfire is alive and ever-changing. It is an experience for all our senses. You could see the many colors and changing shapes of the sticks and logs as they burned to glowing coals. The sounds of the growing fire might also include some pops and hisses as wood or pinecones warmed enough to speak. From a distance, you could smell the invitation to gather around the circle as the scent of the burning wood filled the air. You might taste food enchanted by the fire, whether it was a hot dog, a pot of coffee, or a marshmallow just off the stick. A good fire feels warm on a chilly evening as the logs transform to flame, to embers, and finally, to ashes.

Usually, there is at least one person in the group that can produce a great campfire every time. Their arrangement of the kindling and logs make it start easily and burn well. Others are gifted as fire tenders. Using a long stick or other tool, they poke and prod the fire at just the right time and in just the right place to keep it stirred up. New logs are added so that the flames are fed long enough until those gathered around campfire are done.

When you join a campfire, or even as you drive by a campfire in the distance, the smell can transport you back to another time and place in your earlier story. Such is the power of something that touches all the senses and creates a fond memory.

Every successful campfire needs three ingredients: a lighter, kindling, and wood. The fire depends on enough heat from the lighter to ignite the kindling that will then engage the logs into the burning fire. Being short on matches, sticks, or hardwood will mean some great magic will be required to avoid disappointment. Better to have a good supply of each so that the fire will start, grow, and continue until all are satisfied.

Our lives are like a campfire. We benefit those in our sphere. We have the opportunity to contribute light, warmth, and other benefits to others in our story. No two of us – like campfires – are quite the same. Each of us includes a combination of personal history, talents, education, personality, and style that is unique. We have all met people in the third act of their lives that are dynamic and engaged with those around them. Sadly, we have met others who have lost the joy of life far too soon. That "life fire" within us can continue to burn strong or can become embers far too soon.

As you engage the last third of your life, it is a good time to take a look at your fuel supply. Do you have enough in your woodpile to get you through the changing seasons that await as you approach retirement, retire, and move forward?

Some people have accumulated many resources early in life. A positive home upbringing, early experiences that encouraged you at school, sports, activities, and friendships may have all started your woodpile well. Others have had to work hard to find and add the resources to their lives that were not there as they grew up. Each stage of life will be a time that burns our fuel, but we can add fuel at each stage as well.

Wherever you began and regardless of how well life has gone for you, this is an opportunity to take stock for your future. What fuels our present and our future?

Our friendships have sustained us through the ups and downs of life. We lose friends along the way to distance, changes in our lives, and to their passing on as well. The older we get, the more these old friends will be valuable to us. What are you doing to nurture the old friends who have journeyed with you over your story? How can you stay in touch, spend time, and grow stronger together as you grow older?

What are you doing to add new friends from your generation or the generations that follow? How can you contribute to the lives of others as a friend? Friendship is a great antidote to many of the maladies of aging like loneliness and discouragement. Keeping the old and making new friends is a way to add fuel to keep your fire for life burning strong.

Family continues to be important as we age. Some of your family is gone. New family may be added with you having new or additional titles as parents, grandparents, aunts, uncles, or cousins (however many times removed). Your relatives may be very close to you. Others might play less of a role. Take inventory of those family relationships. How can you strengthen what is there? Are there relationships that have been neglected? Make some phone calls. Study your family tree. Reach out to the long-lost relatives who, like you, might be very happy to reconnect. Send some emails. Invite family to spend time with you. Now is the time to add to that part of your woodpile.

Our physical health reflects many aspects of our journey. In the aging process, our genetic predispositions become more pronounced as we get older. The thousands of little choices in our diet, exercise, and environment start to show their accumulated results for better and for worse. The life experiences of accidents and injuries leave their marks and complications. Do a review of your current health. What choices can you make today and moving forward that will sustain you and help you thrive in the years ahead?

People often extend the concept of "lifelong learning" only as long as their careers will benefit from it. Do not stop there. Learning is another piece of the anti-aging strategy that comes from engaging our minds. Never let your mind retire. Reading, music, drama, and the online world all await you. Creative development through photography, writing, or art can be greatly enriching. Enroll in that university course you never took. Travel as near or far as you can. Stimulate your mind and life. A healthy mind is very valuable in our third act.

The development of our spiritual lives also provides us with fuel for the journey. Nurturing this part of who we are benefits us at every stage. It adds strength in our third act as well. Exploring the meaning and purpose of life is not just for the young. Age gives us a deeper sense of what is most important and how we choose to live through the good and bad times of life. If you are part of a faith community, continue to be involved for its benefit and yours. Keep adding to your spiritual development.

Wise financial decisions continue to be essential as we approach and then journey through our retirement. Many uncertainties in the world around us and in our lives make this very difficult to navigate. Benefit from a good financial plan that is reviewed regularly to meet our changing needs.

One of the dangers people encounter as they grow older is the "familiar trap." We increasingly prefer and rely on what is familiar to us. It requires less adjustment than encountering something new. It also provides a kind of comfort to us. We begin to rely on doing what we have always done to the point that any change becomes distasteful. Try something new and different. Expand your experiences beyond the familiar. Be open to new horizons. You will add flexibility to your personality and your life.

None of us know how many life experiences await us. Some might be grand and wonderful while others may be challenging. Whatever is left in our story, having a well-stocked woodpile means that our life fire will continue to burn strongly in the years ahead. Add to those resources that will fuel your life.

THE RETURN OF WONDER

One of the many benefits of life after retirement is the return of wonder. That great quality we had as children allowed us to find awe and beauty in some of the most common things around us. As children, the exploration of our world involved new sensations that gave us a very long list of firsts in a very short time. The many flavors of food we encounter as children give us some of the variety that life will continue to offer us. Our touch, the sounds we hear, and the smells we encounter all begin to fill in what it means to be alive. Life begins in a small circle of home and family. It gradually grows to neighbors, friends, and extended family. Before long, it is school and our world outside the home that takes hold. In the routines of life, we stop noticing many of the things we had experienced before. It is the new encounters that get our attention. Over time, the rhythm of life reduces something strange and novel to the point that we feel surprise when see something for the first time. Entertainment and internet posts have to find the truly bizarre to get our attention. After all, we have seen it all.

For good reason have people told us to "take time to smell the roses" as we hurry through life. We miss so much that is all around us. Just as parents feel like they will never survive the years of tiny tots, the moments slip away and the children have grown up. Whether you prefer the sentiments of "Turn Around" with the Kingston Trio, "Sunrise – Sunset" sung by Topol or "Cat's in the Cradle" with the voice of Harry Chapin, you know you were told that it would all go by too fast.

The fact that life changes as we get older gives us a renewed opportunity to revisit some of our lost loves. We can reacquaint our senses with the world we missed. A new freedom to explore life has come. We can once again engage in something just because we are interested. It no longer has to meet the requirement of being useful or profitable.

The last third of the journey gives us the freedom to rediscover ourselves. Travel, reading, music, art, and so many other pursuits open us to new worlds that have been waiting to be explored during our time on the treadmill of life.

If you are so fortunate as to live long enough to return to wonder, open your eyes wide and take in the glories of life that were waiting for you all this time.

WIKIS AND WAKES

There are many ways that each of us evaluates our life. You may have had some career goals when you were quite young that have changed over the generations. Not many generations ago, it was common to simply follow in the footsteps of whatever our parents had done. We would continue the family farm or be the blacksmith or baker in our town.

Many baby boomers dreamed of being astronauts. The beginning of the space race, along with the coverage of each adventure of the Mercury, Gemini, and Apollo missions, made it an exciting prospect. Add the wonder of science fiction and children of the 50s and 60s could believe that they too could go where no one had gone before (sadly, it is a challenge for many kids today to find that dream).

Whatever your first dreams were, life may have taken you down some very different roads. The exploration of opportunities at college or university may have introduced new careers. You may have discovered that becoming a physician meant learning organic and inorganic chemistry – that can be a game changer. With the growth of innovation and technology in the sixties, you may have discovered careers that did not exist only a generation earlier.

Your choice of schools, along with what job opportunities were present when you graduated, all contributed to the early course of your career path. As you remember those first jobs, you probably have a blend of nostalgia for the freshness of those new experiences combined with the amazement that you ever had that kind of work. You may wish you had done more of it or are grateful that something else took its place.

Perhaps you graduated from school into a job that you held for most of – or even your entire – career. Share that fact with a twenty-something today, and they will be both amazed and perhaps envious. Our world certainly does not offer that prospect very often now.

That type of career may have offered a great deal of stability and security for you and your family. If you are a parent, you share the concern about the prospects for the next generation who are saddled with massive school debt and facing poor employment prospects. Their stories, as ours were, will be written over the course of their careers. Individual choices will cause twists and turns, as will larger forces in the world's economy.

Many baby boomers look back at their career with amazement that they somehow survived all the uncertainties that surrounded their story. Growing up with the horrors of World War II just behind us, it was a time of opportunity for an expanding peacetime economy. The Korean War and later the War in Vietnam reminded us of how fragile peace was and how close conflict would always be. The backdrop of the Cold War meant that our excitement for a dynamic future was always tempered by the instructions to "duck and cover" in the event of nuclear attack.

Looking forward when we were applying for our early employment, we were taught the value of building our resume. The progress of our careers would be measured on that resume as we continued to add new experiences or responsibilities. Even if we held the same job, it meant that our resume was that much more solid through our consistent work.

Some baby boomers were able to go beyond a resume to achieve something noteworthy in their careers. For some, it was a moment in time when they created, invented, or accomplished something that stood out. Others had responsibilities in politics, business, a profession, or the arts that made their career significant.

The generations of "the great" were recorded in books and biographies. Collections of famed people populate encyclopedias and books of "Who's Who" in the world.

The current record of people of note is Wikipedia, the free online encyclopedia. This collects historical events, places, products, and ideas that are instantly accessible to internet users around the world. To have an entry on Wikipedia denotes that you have some high level of accomplishment in your life. It could be fame, political activity, business success, or a significant contribution to the arts or many other categories. Wikipedia and its ilk are largely populated with the great. Rarely do such places record those we might call "the good."

Often in life, the good are not as newsworthy or particularly gifted as the great. Instead, the good are known by those whose lives they touch with acts of kindness and service. Whether at home, work, in the workplace, or in the community, the good make their important contributions. This is usually in smaller and more subtle ways that are not often measured by any grand event. They serve the poor, sit with a friend who is ill, and have a coffee with someone who is struggling. You can count on them to show up when there is a need for them.

Sometimes, these good people are noticed and thanked. Often, they are not. Where you do hear the truth of their good life and many acts of kindness is at their wake.

At a funeral, you may hear many recitations of accomplishments, and the nature of a eulogy is to praise the person who is no longer with us. That celebration of a life combines with an effort to comfort loved ones and friends in the funeral service.

But the time when you truly learn about the good person comes later. As family and friends gather at a wake, you begin to hear the stories of a life well lived. The tales tell of how that person made a difference in the acts of kindness and care for others. You hear adjectives like affable, friendly, sympathetic, giving, and cheery. The good are remembered for the way their lives touched the lives of others for the better. These were the people who responded to the calls of those in need. Reliable and positive, these were friends who never gave up on those in their lives.

One of the opportunities of later life is to work on how we will be remembered at our wake. No matter our achievements that might be "Wiki-worthy", the difference we choose to make in the lives of those around us may ultimately be more profound and valuable. For those of us who have never had the kind of singular or career achievements to qualify us for a "Who's Who" book, we may find that those who know us value our contributions more than us being one of the greats. Little wonder that many of the greats recognize the need to turn to philanthropy following their success. They recognize that to be known as a good person is of great value too.

Regardless of whether you find yourself at the moment to be in the great or the good, it is a wise thing to take time to share with the good people in your life how they have made a difference for you. Do not wait for their wake to remember their kindness and care.

Be sure to add service of others to your list of how to finish well in the years to come.

BIRDS OF A FEATHER

Visit any diner or donut shop mid-morning and you will not be surprised to see a group of friends gathered around having a chat. The group will seem to be a strange combination of people who are the same and yet different.

They likely will all be around the same age. You might see a five or even ten year difference between the oldest and the youngest in the gathering. What you will also notice, if you're sitting at a table nearby and take the opportunity to watch, is that they have very different personalities. It is usually not a gathering of extroverts or of introverts but the kind of blend that you might expect to find at a workplace or in a community group.

Flocked before you are what are known as birds of a feather. It is a very boomer thing to do, just as it was for the generations that went before.

What type of feather connects them can be as varied as the life stories that each in the group has lived. It could be a group of retirees who made a commitment to keep in touch – and are actually doing it. Some are old or current neighbors who may have raised their children together many years before. It might be friends from a faith community, past or present. Others share a bond of service as to the military.

Earlier generations made gathering together for no other purpose than conversation a convention to be observed. In British pubs, coal miners or academics would find a place where they belonged and would meet regularly to talk together. In Victorian and Georgian England, social clubs were the places where the great and good would gather to discuss matters state and life away from the workplace and the home. These became places and times for ideas to be exchanged and social bonds to be created and reinforced.

You might be able to think of places where your grandparents would gather regularly to be with their friends for a no more complicated purpose than to be together. Whether it was weekly, monthly, or just occasionally, these times were anticipated and were not to be missed. In coming together, the individuals and the group were able to mark the passing of life with the news and shared experiences that were part of growing older. As friends suffered the losses of spouses or other friends, being part of that larger group helped to reinforce a sense of belonging and connection.

Baby boomers are no different in their need to be connected. Some feel it more acutely, depending on the activities and social commitments that are part of their lives. Others are busy enough that it is not something urgent for them at the time. As life changes over time, most will feel the call to flock together with those old friends and colleagues who might be available and willing to get together too.

Whether or not you will have that opportunity may be the result of the choices you make in your 50s and 60s. If you move from the community where you raised your children, you will not have that natural connection. Similarly, if you move away from where you worked, the possibility of being with a group of other retirees may also be reduced.

What you can choose to do at any stage of life is to decide who you would like to have as an old friend. Once you have decided on those people in your life that you think you would enjoy sharing time with over the decades to come, pay attention to those relationships. Invest time in that friendship, even if life takes you miles away. It is much more difficult for all but the most outgoing to find new friends as we get past retirement unless we are gathered in a setting with others who are at the same age and stage.

There are many benefits to gathering together with the other birds who share something in common with us. It is beneficial to have a group of friends who value you as part of the group. The act and art of conversation can give us many social benefits as it keeps us engaged and involved with others. One of the risks of retirement and beyond is the tendency to become more solitary (or, if you are in a relationship, only doing things as a couple), which reduces the opportunities to feed your social needs.

For those in relationships, it can be great to get together with other couples. However, once you lose a spouse, you will find couples' gatherings to be difficult to partake in for many reasons. That's why it is helpful to also have the interaction with a group of friends that is not dependent on your status in a couple.

What feathers do you have that could lead you to be part of a regular gathering of a group of friends? How are those relationships now? Are you doing anything to create times together with those groups that might mutually sustain you and them in the coming years?

So, the next time you see a group gathered together at that coffee shop or bakery, look for the feather that they have in common and celebrate their choice to flock together.

A GOOD SPORT

For most people, a sport is a great connection to a healthier future. While many can enjoy walking, jogging, and running into their later years, many others need to be mentally engaged in the way that a sport requires. What sport is best for you?

We are naturally inclined to sports that we played when we were younger – particularly where we have been successful. As our knees and other joints resist some of the demands of those sports of our youth, we will sometimes find ourselves participating in a master's version of swimming, a friendly game of volleyball, or even a no-hit version of hockey. Much of these alternatives depend on the accumulated injuries that we have sustained over the years along with our general cardio-vascular condition.

Some sports promote a higher level of social interaction while we exercise. Golf, tennis, and bowling can give us moments of activity along with strolls or breaks in between for conversation (and recovery). One of the keys to matching the right sport for your age and stage is to have a good understanding of your current health status. It is important to know your limits and your potential for activity. In consultation with your physician, trainer, and other health professionals, you should be able to describe the activities you have enjoyed in the past, those you currently can do, and those you might want to do again – or for the first time.

Inactivity is certainly a quick ticket to poor health. So is the wrong kind of activity. Discover what is best for you as you review what demands and risks a sport might require and what limits you can set to avoid injury. What is a fact of aging is that we do not recover as quickly from our aches and pains – and especially broken bones – as we did when we were younger.

What we do know is that what you enjoy doing, you are more likely to do again. For some, that's the freedom of a jog, a walk in the forest, or a stroll by the ocean. If going on a hike works for you, make the time to do it.

If those solitary activities do not connect with need for the game, find out what sport is right for you. Talk to your healthcare professionals, find some friends, and get going!

KEEPING BEES

One of the most famous beekeepers in Sussex Downs, England was better known at a different address where many adventures began and were retold. The address is 221B Baker Street in London. That, of course, is the home of the great fictional detective (or is he real by now?) Sherlock Holmes.

The master sleuth, from the imagination of Scotsman and physician Sir Arthur Conan Doyle, captivated audiences in the late Victorian period and continues to enchant readers and audiences today. He was known for his brilliant mind and keen powers of observation. Using the discipline of deductive reasoning, he was able to solve some of the most complex mysteries ever written in the detective genre.

Over the years, the intensity of his efforts took their toll on both his mind and body. He was ready to retire to the countryside. His primary occupation was to change from detecting crime to observing and caring for bees. Actual letters arrived for many years from around the world to the fictional detective at the famous address on Baker Street. Some had questions while others had their own desperate mysteries to solve. They all receive the standard response, "Mr. Holmes has retired to keep bees in Sussex."

Perhaps you too are like Sherlock. Do you look forward to the end of your current job and anxiously await retirement? If you could retire tomorrow, what would be your new occupation – or preoccupation? Is there something that you have always dreamt of doing, if only time had allowed?

For some people, continuing to do what they are doing as long as they physically and mentally can is the quest. For others, they look for that date when the rest of their life awaits to take them to hobbies or interests that have been left untended as the demands of work and family took priority.

Some see travelling as the great deferred pleasure. Others look to painting or writing as the opportunity postponed. A farm, cabin, or cottage may become the place you spend more of your time, leaving the city behind.

What is clear is that having a hobby or interest that engages your mind and soul can bring great satisfaction along with the challenges of learning something new.

So, whatever your dream, plan to enjoy the extra opportunities that come with being retired.

NOTHING TO FEAR

It is remarkable how well the generation before the baby boomers adapted to new technology. Many learn to use email, surf the web, adapt to cell phones, and manage the many complexities of a digital world. We will not mention the inability to set the flashing clock on the VCR since that is something that has eluded most generations. Members of that generation certainly saw great changes during their working lives in technology going from vacuum tubes to transistors to microchips.

The baby boomers grew up in a world exploding with new technologies. Think of any area of life at the end of World War II and compare it to today. This rapid change is on a scale never seen before.

As has always been true, not all of these changes are for the better. Our quality of life and sense of well-being may not be what they once were. If asked, you might find it difficult to decide what technologies you would be willing to discard in favor of what there was in the late 1940s.

Like the racing car driver who is used to seeing the track and other cars moving at 180 mph, baby boomers are up to speed with the idea of change. Changes in technology and life are expected. The risk in retirement is not that technology will leave you behind but that you will opt out.

We have all met people in the workplace who at some point in their careers decided that they were not willing to learn any more. Perhaps it happened when computers were first introduced to their industry. Maybe it began with the need to learn some new software. They would mutter under their breath that they were not going to learn one more thing. With retirement on the horizon, they made the calculation that they could ride out the last months and years.

The resistance to change does increase as we get older. Some of this is in social areas as we try to preserve old ways of thinking and doing. Sometimes older is better, but often it comes down to our comfort level. We become comfortable with the familiar, even when it is not better. The energy to learn becomes more difficult to summon up, and we find ourselves willing to opt out of whatever is next.

The danger of this attitude is that when we decide it is time to stop learning new things, we start to shut down our capability to learn. If you retire at 60 or 65, you may still have 30 years to live. We might not know all the changes that will be ahead of us, but we can be sure that there will be change. If we are out of the habit of learning, it becomes very difficult for us to get those wheels back in motion when we must learn something new.

Learning is believed to be one of the ways to postpone many of the mental problems of aging. People, who are taking on challenges like learning a new language, playing a musical instrument, or even just doing puzzles keep their minds engaged with the flexibility required to learn.

The same flexibility is needed in our social relationships. The willingness to meet and engage new people in our lives also makes us feel better about ourselves and life compared to those who have stopped trying.

With the advance of technology, one of the good trends most products follow is that they start out as a great idea, are engineered for use, and are finally reengineered to be user-friendly. Interfaces like speech recognition make it possible for people of all ages and physical conditions to operate more and more devices. These are especially important innovations for us as we age. The more natural the interface, the more effective we will be when we call on it.

It is easy to imagine a world where many activities will be supported by robotics. Just as robots have made manufacturing more efficient, expect that there will be a wide range of assistive technologies to benefit an aging population. Today's experimental cars that drive themselves are not just something that might make our traffic patterns more efficient. One of the toughest waypoints in aging is losing the ability to drive your car. The loss of independence often means a change in residence and many other new realities. If a car can drive itself, seniors could safely drive to their destination even when their reaction times have slowed due to aging (this is not such good news for taxi drivers, however). The same may be true of many life tasks.

You may be familiar with the early developments in virtual reality. Virtual reality is often mentioned as a great innovation for gaming and engineering since you can experience so much more in the virtual world by wearing the headgear rather than just looking at a flat screen. Architects will be able to "walk through" their buildings before they are built. Think of the applications for seniors who love to travel but face limitations. They could enjoy virtually visiting far off places or dangerous terrain that might be beyond their abilities. Already, virtual reality programs have begun to engage some of these ideas. Baby boomers may be some of the greatest beneficiaries of these advances.

We are the generation that grew up with the science fiction of Star Trek that now is understood to be prescient of what would become science fact in our lifetime. Even the fanciful idea of replicators has found its early expressions in 3-D digital printing that recreates more and more types of objects.

So, do not fear change. Hang on to the tradition of the astronauts and Star Trek of which change is a friend waiting to take you somewhere new and interesting. Welcome the challenges of learning and adapting for your mind's sake. Engage with the new technologies and devices that come along. It has the bonus of making you a cool grandparent.

THE BLACK DOG

Depression has afflicted some of the most gifted and successful people in history. Some had bouts of depression where the fight to feel better seemed to go all fifteen rounds. Others would have a shorter battle. After a while, most who suffer depression come to recognize when it will intensify. For the great Winston Churchill, he described depression as a black dog that would appear and seem to pursue him.

All of us, either personally or with a friend or family member, will ultimately deal with depression. As individuals get older, the likelihood of depression increases significantly. Depression in the elderly is perhaps higher than the already high levels of depression noted in adolescence. The reasons for higher levels of depression include decreasing physical and mental abilities along with increased stress of financial demands. Many individuals live on fixed incomes as they get older. The losses of our parents and close friends and other family members increase as we get older. Ultimately, our independence decreases as we get older. It is important to recognize depression in all age groups, but especially the elderly.

Depression is different from sadness. Sadness is a transient mood that can overtake us at any time as a reaction to a situation or perceived loss. Depression is more of a sustained mood that sets in and does not go away. Depression can manifest itself in many ways. Sometimes the amount of sleep we need seems to increase or, as in many cases with depression, we do not sleep as well. Sometimes individuals wake up early in the morning and cannot get back to sleep. There can be associated feelings of fatigue or despair. Sometimes individuals note increased appetite and weight gain, but more than likely, there is a decrease in appetite that might result in significant weight loss. There is a lack of interest in doing things that we used to enjoy. There is a depressed mood on a daily basis that lasts longer than a couple of weeks. More severe forms of depression can result in feelings of extreme guilt or even suicidal thoughts. Many times, individuals with depression tend to isolate themselves from others because they believe they are a burden to other people if they feel this way.

Do you or someone you know have depression? Are you feeling sad, hopeless, and helpless? If these feelings that are noted in you or in family or friends are more than just sadness, it would be advisable to consult a mental health professional for guidance and treatment. Sometimes individuals with depression just need therapeutic counseling, but other times, in more severe forms of depression, psychiatric medications are needed such as antidepressants and mood stabilizers. It is important when dealing with depression to get plenty of rest. It is also important to avoid alcohol and to eat healthy foods. One way to help with depression is to exercise at least three times weekly. It does not have to be heavy exercise; even walking outside three times a week for at least 30 minutes at a time can be helpful for your body. Sometimes, going on vacation and getting away from surrounding stressors can be a helpful thing to do. Even though an individual with depression many times does not feel like it, it is important to reach out to others and let them know what is going on so they can help out. You might be surprised at how willing friends, family members, and mental health professional are to provide help and support. Depression can be a very frustrating illness. It is a medical illness that is treatable just like other medical illnesses including diabetes and high blood pressure. As newer treatment options emerge year by year, it is important to recognize, identify, and treat all forms of mood disorders. You do not have to go through this alone.

TIME & TREASURE

We have lived in the past few generations with the idea that we would outlive our money and have some left to pass along to the next generation. Like many things between the generations of the 1900s, times have changed.

As the parents of baby boomers pass away, some will have funds left over to give the next generation a boost. Increasingly, many of that previous generation finds that with the increased medical costs, this is no longer a certainty. Many estates are drained by the medical expenses in the last months of life. It is a terrible dilemma to face the choices that suddenly appear when you are not well. Physicians and families struggle with the expectations of how to prolong life with one more treatment or possibility. As it relates to our finances, people face the balance between time and treasure. How much treasure shall I spend for what may or may not be extra time?

Reduced equity in investments in an ever-changing real estate or stock market can also interrupt the best-laid plans for retirement. Many people are also learning that the pensions they earned at work may not survive corporate bankruptcies or mismanagement. Benefits and payments that might have been expected in retirement can be caught in the cross-fire of city, state, and creditors.

Another large factor for many families currently is the presence of low interest rates. While low rates are helpful for a faltering economy and beneficial for those seeking a mortgage, they reduce the income for those who use interest earning investments for their retirement savings. While the first priority of savings is to beat the inflation rate, interest investments often do not receive any tax preferences when compared to dividend and capital gains income. Interest investments have the benefit of being more stable and reliable (depending on the underlying savings investment), but often they lose ground after inflation and taxes are factored into the story. As a result, generations that have preferred to save using interest paying savings accounts, money markets, or bonds may find themselves gradually falling behind year after year. Over the short term, this is not a big problem, but if you have the opportunity to live a couple of decades beyond your three-score and seven years, this becomes a factor.

In addition to healthcare, many seniors move from their homes to various levels of residential care. It may begin as a seniors' condo or village; then, with increasing need for care and support, it may develop into a care facility. Unless you qualify for subsidized care, that can become a large expense.

One of the many advantages of staying in your home is the opportunity for your home's equity to continue growing for a longer period of time, assuming that the real estate market in your area is on the upswing. There are many other advantages to staying in your home. Whether that works for you and how long you can remain at home safely depends on what kind of community and family support might be available.

Everyone approaching retirement would benefit from a financial review. As you may live for decades after retirement, it is important to match your investments to known health and financial obligations. Using an independent financial advisor who can give you objective advice that is customized to you is very helpful.

Money can be a source of stress at any time of life. It can go from being a stress to an obsession as we get older. Be sure that your retirement financial plan matches your goals and expectations for your retirement years. Develop a sense of how much treasure over what period of time will be required.

It is also important to match the risk of your investments not only to the time that the investment will have to grow, but also how much risk you can tolerate as you get older. Many people who are making excellent returns over a five or ten year period using stocks and other equity investments cannot enjoy a single day of it. That is because they live with the fear that tomorrow it may go down. They then extrapolate to the next fear that they will lose it all.

Make sure that your financial advisor knows what keeps you awake at night when it comes to money. Not having enough money will be a stress; making money in an unpredictable way can be a stress as well. Use a financial advisor who is recommended not just for the great results she or he can bring their clients but also whether they have the ability to listen carefully to what is important to you.

Of course, it is great if you set aside tidy sums of money each year from your first paycheck onward. For many people, life was not that predictable or forgiving.

Whatever your situation today, start planning the balance of time and treasure now.

JUST ONE MORE THING...

Columbo was a beloved TV show of the late 1960s that extended with television specials until 2003. It remains a popular show in syndication.

Peter Falk played the detective and endeared himself to audiences over many generations. With his disheveled hair, beat up Peugeot 403 Cabriolet, and rumpled trench coat, he seemed an unlikely choice to investigate murders of the rich and famous. His charm was found in his self-deprecating humor, gentleness, and easy smile. His adversaries usually underestimated him until it was too late.

One of Lt. Columbo's tactics was to conclude a conversation with the suspect and begin to walk away. With his adversary's guard now down, Columbo would turn back with a finger raised in the air. Then he would make the inevitable statement, "Just one more thing, sir." That usually led to an opportunity for Columbo to disclose something he knew by way of a question or to mention an inconsistency that had no good answer except to point to their part in the crime.

People with great people skills and many friends have learned the value of asking that "one more thing" in a conversation.

So much of our time is spent minimizing our contact with others. We say the bare minimum when ordering in a line. Many find their dating relationships through an online service. We try to be concise in our texts and emails – already a far cry from the letters we used to write a generation ago. Many people have lost the art of conversation as can be seen at many formal or other social gatherings. Even our greetings like "How are you?" are so routine that the person being asked is quite sure that you do not really want an answer to that. Perhaps we learn this first when parents ask their children, "How was school today?" only to receive the perfunctory answer of "Fine."

Imagine if you took the time in your close relationships, family connections, or even new acquaintances to ask one more thing?

That extra question might give you a new insight into that person's story. The best choices are those "open-ended" questions that are not typically answered with a yes or no but instead have many possible answers. An open-ended question allows the other person to share something (or not) as they wish. But the very act of asking the person communicates that you are open to a conversation with them beyond the bare minimum that passes for civil in our society.

Questions can be as simple as "What's new with you?" or "How is life treating you?" People with high SQ (the social skills equivalent to IQ for intelligence) pay attention to what they already know about people they have met. They will use times together or other communication to refer to something specific about the person so that the person again has an opportunity to respond. "How is your daughter doing at university?" "How does your son like his new job?" "What are you doing now that you are retired?"

Asking that one additional thing invites the person to engage with you on a deeper level. They may have something positive to share, it may relate to a burden they are carrying, or they may tell you something you never knew about them. In each case, you are making a deeper connection with that person. Before long, they will likely ask you something about your world. This give and take is a key element of making deeper friendships.

Developing deeper relationships is especially important to people as they age. We spend much of our youth inheriting relationships from our family and forming relationships with our friends. Some of these will grow into lifelong friendships that provide the companionship and fellowship that help us go through our lives. As we get older, some of those family members and friendships will no longer be available to us as we move around and as death separates us from them. That means that we need to be in the business of making friends and being social as we get older.

While some people are more extroverted and enjoy large social gatherings, some are quite content with a small collection of close friends. It is the introverts who have to continue to practice their friendship skills since losing someone from a large group of friends is not as devastating as it would be to lose one of your few companions. Often, introverts are more reluctant to be social in the first place. Loneliness in retirement and beyond makes it very difficult to finish well.

The older you are, the more intentional you must be about being friendly and making friends. The settings where we typically made our friends like high school, college, or the workplace are not there for many as they get older. Our loss of social flexibility also makes it easier for us to miss opportunities we might have grabbed when we are younger. Community groups, faith-based gatherings, golf, and other fitness programs also provide opportunities to be with and make friends.

So, regardless of your age and stage, ask that one more thing of the people you encounter. You never know when you will be adding a new friend who will enrich your life as you invest in theirs.

FAMILY OF CHOICE

The old saying, "God chose your family so you could choose your friends" is either a celebration of providential selection or the blessing of a different circle of unrelated people, depending on your family tree.

With life giving children and parents the opportunity or sometimes necessity – to move around much more than in previous generations, families often find themselves separated from older generations, siblings, and offspring. The result is visits on occasional weekends, Skype sessions, phone calls, emails, or text messages. An important element of society, the clan, or family group, is now separated. The supports and challenges of those relationships are now irregular and fragmented. More than just missing the advantages of built-in babysitters or grandchildren-to-go, the loss of everyday connection can leave some significant gaps.

In places like the United States, Canada, Australia, and New Zealand, this is not an entirely new phenomenon as these countries were largely populated by immigration. Elder members of the family left behind their "old countries" to escape famines, lack of opportunity, or sometimes persecution in the hopes of a better life somewhere else. New immigrants tend to collect in communities where there are others from their background. The social bonds in these communities allow for the celebration of their heritage and to forge new relationships based on their original language and history. As the next generations grow up, there is usually a resistance to continuing with the first language and cultural ties as they integrate into their new country and its social structure. It is often the third or fourth generation that begins to once again reconnect with the family's culture of origin.

The expectation and acceptance that the family will all live in proximity to one another diminishes over the generations. Children and grandchildren often face the same need to find education or work as the earlier generations did. The older generations are less likely to move and uproot their social structures. Sometimes however, the retirees choose to move to a better climate or a less expensive area of the country to live. It is not surprising to find some or all of a family living miles apart.

While not minimizing the value and importance of staying connected with our kith and kin when we can, when distance is involved, it might be time to consider a family of choice. This is especially true for people without children or who have lost parents and siblings along the way.

The family of choice is a decision to add to your existing family new relationships that will fill in some of the social gaps in your life. This is not a new series of legal relationships; instead, it is a process of creating opportunities to share life experiences with compatible people from different generations.

With the loss of our parents and older family members, we become the oldest generation in our family. It is helpful to reach out to seniors who are of the earlier generation. True throughout life, it is always valuable to be in touch with those who have been on the journey longer that you have. The insights and perspectives that older people can share will often give you hope when it seems like life is not working for you. They can also affirm you as you face the stages of retirement and aging that they have already experienced. The wisdom from their years on the road can be invaluable to someone a few laps behind. It can be a bonus to connect with older folks who were friends of your parents and extended family. We tend to see and know our older generation through the lens of family. Those who knew them as friends or colleagues can give you a wider perspective on what your family members were like in the past or as friends. That can give you a different point of view of them and you. When your parents are gone, you learn that it is still helpful to find those who will take on that parent-friend role to support you in your journey.

Siblings and cousins grow in importance as we grow older. As distance or death takes them away, adding friends who can share that type of fraternal friendship is a strength as we age. These deeper friendships take work because we do not have the many shared experiences from childhood and youth that our siblings had with us.

Beyond the previous and same generations, we also benefit by connecting with the younger generations. This might be by befriending a family in the neighborhood with a younger family or through church, sports, or other areas of life. Being available to participate in another family through a BBQ or offering support when someone is sick or has a loss gives that younger family a greater opportunity for their future life. Just as older friends can give us perspectives on life, we can help the next generation with assurances that they too will get through this challenging stage. As is true in so many spheres of life, our willingness to encourage others often leads to our own encouragement along the way.

So, if you have gaps in your current family structure by geography, conflict, or loss, seek the opportunity to add to your family of choice to enrich your life through the benefits of trans-generational friendships.

GENERATION NEXT

Built into the social fabric of each generation is a commitment to the next. This can be understood on many levels. Take care of the generation that follows so the species will continue. Encourage a healthy and strong generation to follow so that the society in which you will be old and more vulnerable functions well. Altruistically giving to the next generation propagates the gifts we received from the generations before us. Self-sacrifice is a noble quality that serves the best interests of others and makes a positive statement of who we are. For our legacy, the next generation is part of our immortality.

Passing on wisdom to the next generations also appears to be part of what it means to be human. Developmental psychologist Eric Erikson described the social development of people based on the stages that each person must normally experience. At each stage, a person is faced with a challenge that may be answered positively or negatively. The first stage is trust vs. fear. Will I assume that I can trust the new world I am encountering, or should fear be the normal reaction? These early answers form much of the patterns we will experience over our lifetimes.

Skip down to stage seven and you encounter the terms generativity vs. stagnation. The healthy choice that opens us to a better future is generativity. Choosing stagnation is to stifle our future.

This is a stage of middle adulthood typically between ages 40-65. Individuals have an internal need to create or nurture that which will live longer than they will.

Parents experience this in later years with their growing and grown children. The period of launching your children into adulthood is different from those years when they are dependent. Their future starts to be defined by their interests and choices of college, work, and relationships. They start to look like a generation rather than just children. Regardless of whether or not you have children, generativity is a stage that calls to each one to pay it forward by serving those who are following.

Rather than being focused on your own success, moving into the stage of generativity means that you want to make the world a better place for the generations that follow. That can include mentoring, nurturing, and supporting individuals in your life. Participation in your local community or faith group becomes an expression of this care for others. It might also been seen on a larger scale in your care for causes in our world greater than yourself to improve the quality of life and opportunity for the next generation.

It is essential that we do not disconnect ourselves from our communities and societies and the world. This is very important for good mental health. The alternative at this stage is to be focused on the self, leading to stagnation. We do not recognize or act on the need to contribute to the generation to come. Individuals who do not make that needed connection to those younger than us may feel uninvolved with life as a whole and ultimately might develop clinical depression or anxiety. Those individuals who feel successful during this stage of development usually have a better sense of well-being and fewer tendencies towards mood disorders.

The next (and final) stage in Erikson's is integrity vs. despair. As with all the stages Erikson observed, choosing well in the earlier stage leads to a better next one. This final stage is where people reflect on the meaning of their life. Imperfect as every life always is, those who can look back on their life with a sense that it was worthwhile have a sense of integrity: "It was good to be alive and I made a difference." Those who were self-centered instead reach a different conclusion. They look in the rear-view mirror of life and see that it has all passed them by. Not measured by the size of the bank account or the accolades received, those who have spent their life investing in others thrive at the journey's end. Those who have served only themselves despair.

It is a privilege to share and encourage the life of someone from the next generation. Taking the opportunity to make our community and the world a better place is an important choice to make. If you are feeling that tug to make a difference for generation next, do not allow yourself to stagnate. Connect with the next generation individually and as a community. Choose generativity. It will help them and you have a better tomorrow.

BREAKING THE CHAINS

The power to forgive is a great gift we have all been given but seldom use. Many do not realize that they have this essential ingredient for keeping relationships healthy.

The damage to relationships caused by the stresses and strains of life, combined with our many careless moments, leave us all with many scars.

From our most casual encounters to our most intimate relationships, we find many ways to let down and hurt those we hardly know, those we love dearly, and those who are somewhere in between. This means we all have large and small offenses, both real and imagined, that consume our thoughts and emotions. Friends, family members, spouses, employers, colleagues, neighbors, and strangers can offend us at any moment. Sooner or later (usually sooner), someone will cross our boundary.

Even those of us not gifted in accounting or organization have an amazing ability to calculate and file all of these offenses committed against us. We will even count those actions that were not done that we think should have been. Sins of commission and omission are all fair game. Like a high-speed computer, we can access these files at a moment's notice with all the gory detail included, like a paparazzi account where nothing is left out. As soon as we hear the person's name or see their face, it is all right there. Our muscles tighten and our fists clench at the thought of those who have wronged us again and again. Before long, we start to resemble the bitter old people we used to notice with curiosity when we were children.

The good news is that bitterness is not inevitable. There is a cure for our anger and hurt. The answer is in the power to forgive, something that we all have been given. It is the power to be free from the chains of painful and damaged relationships.

One of the common misconceptions when we talk about forgiveness is that it is better not to forgive: "That person does not deserve to be forgiven" or "What they did to me was so painful or hurts so much that I don't want to forgive them. I refuse."

That misses the point of the gift we have received with forgiveness. Forgiveness is primarily for the benefit of the person doing the forgiving.

Yes, there are certainly some benefits for someone who has been forgiven, and that is important, too. But the first and principal benefit comes to the person who is willing to forgive. That's why we call it the power to forgive: When you choose to forgive, you are actually exercising your power in that relationship to move it forward and to take away the chains that very quickly surround a broken relationship.

Now, to be clear, forgiveness is not the same as justice. So, we are not talking here about crimes. This is not about something in the workplace or community that's inappropriate, illegal, or against company policy. Those justice or legal issues have to be dealt with appropriately through the proper authorities.

This is not hiding the facts about something that is going on that is wrong or illegal. We are not talking about that at all. If a crime was committed, the authorities need to be notified. If it is something that violates company policy, that needs to be dealt with through the proper human resource channels or other authorities.

Forgiveness is about how we process our feelings on the personal side. If you take time to investigate an old hurt, you often discover that the person who hurt you often does not remember, never knew, or does not care about all the churning and turmoil created in your life. Now, that may be the case for a number of reasons. It could be because they did not intend to do anything or did not plan on doing anything to hurt the other person. Perhaps it was neglect, or maybe it was a lack of sensitivity. Often, they do not have any memory of it because it wasn't something that ever appeared on their radar.

For the person who has accumulated this long list of grievances, it may come as a great shock. They have spent plenty of time going over and over this person's faults. The injured party who did nothing to offend them is bitter and upset. Yet, the person who has offended them may not even remember the vexing experience.

All that energy is being spent on someone who was ignorant of the offense or who does not care to have a positive relationship with us. The potential joy and good of that relationship is lost over something they never knew. That is a tragedy.

Of course, there are things that are very legitimate where a person did something to undermine the relationship to hurt us. They might have worked to sabotage something in our life or have done something that was very terrible. This is not minimizing those kinds of actions, as they can be very real. Even with the most intentional hurts by someone against us, it is still in our best interest to forgive that other person. Without forgiveness, that person will always have a negative link to us.

We cut that negative connection by saying, "I am choosing to forgive that person." It does not deny your pain or claim that what happened did not happen. It does not assume that they deserved forgiveness, asked to be forgiven, or are available to ask as they moved away or even died.

It begins by making a decision—not because you feel like doing it. You choose to forgive to set yourself free.

If someone has offended you, it might be helpful to share that with them. This of course depends on the nature of the relationship. Someone you will never expect to see again is probably not a good candidate to meet.

However, if it is a colleague, family member, or friend, it might be worth the effort to let them know how you are feeling. Done well and taken well, it can strengthen a relationship and avoid further conflict arising from careless behavior.

This should not be done as an ambush. It is best if it can be done in a neutral, casual setting like a coffee shop over a cup of coffee or iced tea. The point of going beyond your choice to forgive is to rebuild the relationship. This needs to be shared carefully and with a humble approach.

Ask if they would be willing to meet to discuss something that has been bothering you that you want to put behind you.

If you have such a relationship that they are willing to meet with you, think about what and how you are going to share your feelings. You might say, "I don't know if you are aware of this, but the other day when you said this (or you did that), it really hurt me. I really felt awful about that, and it's been bothering me. I just wanted to talk to you to see if we can work that out."

Hopefully, that other person will say, "Wow, I had no idea. I didn't know this was something between us to talk about, sort out, or apologize for. Will you forgive me?" Then, you can move on with that relationship. That's really the ideal, if that's possible.

It doesn't always work that way, though. Sometimes, the other person is not available or willing to do that. They may wonder what all the fuss is about and just say that they did nothing wrong. Remember, you can still choose to forgive that person even if they do not ask to be forgiven or are unwilling to meet.

Do not be surprised if they use the occasion to bring up something that may have been bothering them about you. Do not interpret that as getting even. It is probably a sense that since you are dealing with uncomfortable topics, you might as well get that out of the way, too. Be prepared to ask for their forgiveness. Remember, like them, you may not have intended offense or even remember it, either. A humble attitude is required for the sake of moving the relationship back on track.

Just as we receive our fair share of offenses, even the most careful people will offend their co-workers, friends, and family. You can always own up to your mistakes or missed opportunities by going to the person as soon as possible and acknowledging what happened. You will find most people are surprised that you would take the risk of doing that. They will respect the fact that you can not only recognize your mistakes but admit them, too.

So many people lose their energy, robbed of their vitality and their sense of the joy of life by these bitter feelings. Even beyond forgiving, it is possible to forget, as well. That may sound impossible and you may be tempted to say, "I will forgive, but I won't forget!" That also keeps you from the more complete experience of moving past those things that hold us back.

The next time you are reminded of what they did to offend you, practice forgiveness. Say, "Yes, I choose to forgive that person." Maybe you will see them across the table or at a meeting. Say to yourself, "I choose to forgive." By that practice, you choose to move on, and that is very liberating. So, one of the things that we encourage you to do is just to get into that practice of forgiving.

If you get into the habit and practice of choosing to forgive, you will be surprised to find out that you really can also forget as well. That gives you the freedom to break the chains and move on to become your best self.

THERE'S NO PLACE LIKE HOME

One of the most emotional transitions to face is the move away from the family home. This might be a planned down-sizing to a smaller place or somewhere with fewer stairs. Maintenance over the winters and summers may have become too difficult. For many people, it is not a choice they would make. Changes in health or the loss of a spouse sometimes mean that it is time to move on.

On one level, we might wonder why it is such a big deal. It is only bricks and mortar or timber and nails. It is not you. A little reflection quickly reminds us why this can be so hard, even when it makes sense.

Our homes are where we make memories. Depending on how long you lived in your current place, you may have raised your children in that home. The house is a witness to the lives lived within it. While the walls can not speak (probably for the best sometimes), we might like to once again hear the sounds of the small voices coming from our young children. Hallway entrances that are now neat and tidy once were littered with many pairs of shoes, fresh off the little feet that ran in them.

Sounds of dinnertime chaos still echo somewhere in those walls. The challenges of ensuring that each person was at their school or sporting event on time were part of those days. The many firsts can happen in a family home. First steps and starting kindergarten suddenly become proms and high school graduations. The grass where small children played became a sporting field for baseball and football. Scrapes, bruises, and other childhood traumas can be marked in and around the residence. Blaring television sets with cartoons give way to laughter at the latest YouTube video.

The house has been a place where you all belonged. If life included many moves, your memories may be fragmented between different places. Memories are often made where we do our living, and home is such a place.

If you are in a position to make the move by choice, it is often a bit easier. It helps to be able to rationally decide that it is the right time for the move and that the change will have many benefits. Do not be surprised if your head and heart diverge when it comes time for the move.

When a person is forced to move due to changes in health or finances, this can be a very intense time. The loss of one's home becomes yet another disappointment in a time when it seems like you are losing the ability to make the choices you wish you could make. It is a loss of independence as well as a departure from a place full of so many memories.

Many healthcare programs recognize the benefits of being able to stay in your home as long as possible. By providing in-home support, there is less strain on the system already struggling to adapt to the bulge of baby boomers beginning to need more healthcare services.

When is it time to move? That has a different answer for each person or couple asking it.

There are some common considerations. First of all is whether or not you are safe. If your health or the configuration of your home does not allow you to live there safely, then it is time for a move.

Are you alone too much? Particularly after the loss of a spouse, the comfortable and cozy home can feel large and empty if you live there by yourself. If you are unable to get out socializing regularly, then home can become a prison.

Do the routines of keeping up the house become too difficult to maintain well? Do you have people in your life like family, friends, or neighbors who can help you with the lawns and snow? In such a case, it can work. Can you resist the temptation to get on the ladder that you promised your children not to climb? Injuries from a fall can dramatically and sometimes permanently change your quality of life.

If you are a couple, how will either of you manage if one of the partners is no longer there? What might work as a shared load may not be something that one or the other of the spouses could handle on their own.

If that is the case, it is helpful to consider a move to a lower maintenance or smaller place while you are still together. That allows memories to start being made in the new place while you are still together and can enjoy it. It is exponentially more difficult to lose a partner and then have to leave your home as well.

Before you face this, you will probably have to deal with the sale of your parent's home. Whether it is through a planned move or due to a death, it is a difficult experience to say goodbye to what was your home too. If the last of your parents is gone, dismantling the home takes away the notion that they might still be there in that familiar setting. You will no longer be able to imagine them coming around the corner or stepping in the house again from the back yard.

People spend part or most of a lifetime turning a house into a home. When we say goodbye to it, that home once again becomes just a house. There is little reason to wonder why it makes us sad to leave. If you listen carefully, you will hear the old house sigh too.

THE BEST MEDICINE

Humor is a gift that can be shared alone, with a friend, in a group, or around the world. A great sense of humor is especially helpful as we age.

There are many aspects of aging that are no fun. Humor will not make all the aches, pains, and losses of aging go away. The older we get, the better developed our sense of humor can be. After all, we have heard jokes and seen funny things in life and entertainment for decades. Finding what is funny in life can make you feel many years younger. It can also be a gift to share with those around you, too.

As we all age, it is important not to take ourselves seriously. I think it is perhaps a natural process because you realize as you get older that there are some things that are more important than others. You also understand that there is only a certain amount of time left to do the things that you want or need to do with your life. All of us begin to recognize our mortality. For many, this begins in the 50s.

While some focus on the negatives of aging such as declining physical health, loss of family and friends, and sometimes the loss of financial freedom, others look at life differently. Growing older helps you identify the true sources of joy and happiness that come each day. Looking on the brighter side often includes seeing the funny side, too.

Opportunities to be with people who are important to us as we grow older mean that we can enjoy their company and hopefully their stories. For many people, the aging process helps us reduce the painful moments to a distant memory as we experience anew the happy and funny memories from our lives. This is especially true if we have been practicing a positive attitude over the decades and if we have learned to forgive those in our lives who have disappointed us. All of that gives us more room for humor and joy.

The same things that can make some people angry can make others laugh as they see the silliness in many of life's moments. Those who have a default for humor will not just wonder if the glass is half empty or half full but perhaps who it was drinking from the glass and why they stopped half way through! Many funny possibilities can be imagined.

Humorous situations are all around us as many comedians like Jerry Seinfeld have proven. His humor was based on seeing the funny things in everyday life. What is routine can be funny if you pause to look at it. It is all part of coming from the human race.

Being humorous does not mean that you are minimizing people's grief or loss or tragic news. There are times to be serious and empathetic. But a light touch that comes from a positive worldview is helpful to those on a dark road as well.

Continue to be caring and kind towards others, but be aware of elements of humor in life as they can ultimately help people feel better about themselves and others.

Have some funny stories at the ready. Watch for the funny side of life. It will give you added vitality and make you someone others will enjoy being around.

After all, someone with laugh lines is much more attractive than someone with frown lines at any age!

OVER THE RAINBOW

For those who love sentimental music, one of the great songs comes from the classic 1939 movie, "The Wizard of Oz." The song "Somewhere Over the Rainbow" is featured in the opening scenes of the story and is sung by Judy Garland. It comes after her character, the teenager Dorothy, has been trying to be heard by the others on the farm who are busy with the chores and challenges of everyday life.

Dorothy was fearful of the nasty neighbor, Miss Gulch. She wanted to do away with Dorothy's faithful dog, Toto. The practical Aunt Em tells her not to imagine things and get herself into a fret over nothing. She is finally told to help them by going somewhere to a place where she will not get into any trouble.

Frustrated, she asks Toto if there could be such a place. If so, she concludes that you would not get there by boat or train. It's "far, far away – behind the moon – beyond the rain."

Dorothy sings this melody that describes how she longs to be somewhere else where blue skies replace the clouds and where her troubles are melted away like lemon drops. If only she could be like the bluebirds who fly over the rainbow. She wants to follow the dreams that she dares to dream – and see them come true. Trouble, of course, was only moments away as Miss Gulch arrives on her bicycle to take Toto away to be destroyed.

One of the challenges of growing older is a feeling that all of your dreams are already used up. In our youth, life seems to be full of so many possibilities. We can dare to dream big dreams because a long future invites us to take the risks. Time and our life journey knock some of those dreams down with a thud. We begin to realize that our talents, experience, and opportunities may mean that we will not find our life over the rainbow as we saw it as teenagers.

With the passing of time, we may be grateful that we did not get what we had hoped for, in retrospect. We may have followed our dreams and gone beyond those aspirations. Maybe there are still dreams that are unfulfilled, but they do not seem totally out of reach.

Dorothy was lamenting being somewhere that she wished she was not. It did not mean that she did not love her Aunt Em and Uncle Henry. She enjoyed the farm hands that had such entertaining personalities. What she felt was lacking was moving beyond her troubles. She felt the dark shadow of Miss Gulch. Toto was at risk. Dorothy was also ready for adventure. She wanted to leave behind that comfortable home to explore the great world beyond.

Age and experience do give us perspectives on those things that crowded our thinking in our youth. We can look back and wonder how what others thought of us mattered so much. The school tests and assignments that struck fear in our hearts no longer seem as formidable. We sometimes muse about what it would be like to go back to those days to relive them. What might we have done differently, if we knew then what we know now? Would we have made the same mistakes or just different ones? Would we really be better off?

What geography of the world or the soul have you not explored because of the responsibilities of life and work? Are the retirement years the time when you will break free to discover the dreams that have been deferred until now?

Those dreams that we have from our youngest years have amazing endurance. They can be tenacious, always nudging us not to forget them. Some of these dreams have always felt "over the rainbow" while others appeared to almost be in our grasp.

Perhaps you have been afraid to dream, not willing to be disappointed again. You may feel that the best years are behind you, so why bother dreaming now?

Whatever your age and stage in life, give yourself permission to dream. You might be pleasantly surprised at how many possibilities are awaiting you if you will watch for them. Dreams were never safe when we were young. You may have ignored your dreams because you were not ready or willing to take the necessary risk. In our later years, sometimes people decide that they are not going to take any more risks. They believe that there is not enough time or they have too much to lose to take on one of their dreams. Instead, use the wisdom and experience that comes with your age to discover new ways to follow your dreams.

With a song in your heart and a companion for the journey, there is no telling what kind of road awaits you. You may indeed yet travel over the rainbow and learn to follow your own yellow brick road to Oz. You will no doubt meet characters along the way who may enrich your life or at least become part of the tales you will later tell.

Like Dorothy, you may find that following your dreams gives you a new appreciation of what is most important. The people in our lives and the familiar places become more valuable as we get older.

As she so eloquently said, "There is no place like home."

STATE OCCASIONS

Families have different traditions that define which social gatherings qualify as a "state occasions" that require our attendance. As we get older, we may come to love these opportunities to connect with family and friends. We may have the opposite reaction, based on our personality or previous experiences with such events.

As a retired person, you will find that some of the easy excuses like being at work are no longer available to dodge one of "those" times.

While family gatherings, weddings, and retirement parties might have differing levels of potential social stress, many retirees find funerals the most difficult. Many dislike funerals at the best of times in their adulthood. They can be celebrations of a long life well-lived. Often, however, they are unexpected losses or the final act of a long struggle. Grieving spouses and emotional family members make a visitation or funeral service challenging to endure. It is natural to want to avoid uncomfortable social times.

The older we get, the more this is true. We begin to associate anyone's death with our growing realization that we too will face our mortality. We also know that we are on a steady march to the end of our story. When there is a death of a peer in our youth by accident or illness, we are shocked and saddened, but we understand that it is not normal. We are still in our invincible years. Others who leave us in our 20s, 30s, and 40s also have the "far too young" connotation, but the increasing frequency starts to hint at our mortality. As cancers and heart attacks take some of our 50s and 60s circle, we take comfort in the statistics that show the average population living longer.

Some enter retirement and leave it quickly. All the plans that awaited the conclusion of the working years will remain unfinished because that life ends. We mourn for those spouses who have just had their golden years together cancelled.

Combined with whatever additional health concerns that have bubbled up in our lives, attending a funeral becomes more and more daunting.

So why put yourself through that kind of "state occasion?"

People who are grieving have many different stages through which all will pass – sooner or later. The road of grief can sometimes be delayed or deferred but not without a cost. Grief is a painful friend to know. But this sadness is a friend who will help us as we allow the stages of grief to run their course.

In her 1969 book, On Death and Dying, Swiss-American Psychiatrist Elisabeth Kübler-Ross identified these stages: denial; anger; bargaining; depression, and finally, acceptance.

Being available to people who are facing a great loss in their life, like the death of a spouse or close friend, is very valuable. The awareness of not being alone in the loss is a powerful antidote to the feelings of despair that can follow a death. Whether it was a long-term illness or a sudden departure, it is always a shock. Having people who surround you and your family at a funeral is a kindness and blessing to the grieving individuals.

Attending a funeral also models compassion for the generations that follow. Funerals can be a bitter-sweet time – bitter as you recognize the loss but also sweet as you honor the life lived and the family they leave behind.

At some point, it will be you or your family who will need that support. Creating communities that not only celebrate birthdays and anniversaries but that also demonstrate compassion at funerals benefits everyone. It may not be easy, but it is very valuable.

In funerals, as with any family "state occasion," stories can provide a deep and powerful benefit to all who are there. At Thanksgiving, holidays, family reunions, weddings, picnics, and retirement parties, stories are the therapy that keeps relationships connected.

Telling stories of the person now gone brings them alive in memory. Co-workers and friends may have stories to tell of how the person made a difference in their lives. Perhaps it was acts of kindness, a great sense of humor, or being a great friend when that was needed. Hearing these stories comforts a grieving spouse or family member and may give them new or additional insight into the loved one they now miss so dearly.

For the children or grandchildren of someone who has passed on, learning new things about their loved one gives them a new understanding of how that person was perceived and appreciated by their peers or colleagues. We tend to know our family members only through the family lens with the intimacy and closeness of our relationship. Unless we have seen them at work or in other contexts, we may not know that side of them that made them a great person during their youth as neighbors in the workplace or the community. Being willing to share your stories about the person with those who remain is a gift of grace that you can give to those who are grieving.

As with most things in life, when you help others, you tend to benefit more than those you seek to encourage. By sharing stories of others, you often find you are touched by the memories too.

But none of this happens unless you show up.

So, the next time you learn that someone you knew well has died, consider the state occasion as an investment in those grieving, your community, and ultimately in your future and the needs of your family when the time arises.

Treat the "state occasion" as a "command performance" and everyone will be better for it.

TUG OF WAR

One of the tests for any generation is how it treats the one that is older as well as how it serves the one coming behind it. Baby boomers have become familiar with not just the phrase but the reality of "the sandwich generation" as they get older.

Longer-lived parents with gradual declines in their health over many years have meant that boomers are caring for an older generation for much longer. Not long ago, it was common for an aging parent to live with their children. With improved programs and care, more seniors can stay in their homes for longer periods of time. This positive development does not always recognize that many of those over 80 can live on their own at home without some consistent involvement of one or more of their children.

Those visits include the emotional and social support as well as filling in some of the gaps in tasks that they cannot do. This might be buying the groceries, caring for bills, or doing some of the chores. If the parent cannot drive, it may also mean taking them to physician appointments and other places to access services. While some home support is available, it is often not enough.

Where there is a loss of independence due to physical or mental health changes, there can be an increasing dependence on the time and participation of children before the senior receives the higher level of support of a retirement home or other care facility.

This tug at the heart and resources of the boomer can be very strong. Many feel that they are not doing enough and experience a sense of guilt. Others are doing all that they can and may find themselves feeling resentful toward the situation, if not the person, that now requires more and more of their attention. Each one deals with the tension of wanting to be there for the parents who raised them and sacrificed along the way while trying to maintain their independence.

Some parents want to be as self-sufficient as possible while others through their grief, depression, or personality patterns want their children to be there for them all the time. They may have many fears of being alone or being vulnerable.

On the other end of the rope, boomers have children who tug them to a greater or lesser extent well beyond their college years. The days of going to university, graduating, getting a good job, and then marrying and having children seem as old as a 1950's rerun of "Leave it to Beaver." The lack of jobs for many graduates means that they may continue their education further, take work that is insufficient to establish their financial future, and often return home to live. High student debt, tight credit, and the lack of opportunities means that many cannot afford to rent, much less buy, accommodations. Boomer parents are torn between wanting their children to be independent while recognizing that this can be very difficult for many boomer children to achieve.

How do boomers balance between the needs of these two forces that pull at their hearts, finances, and time?

Each situation is different and changing. What can be a helpful approach is to consider the following strategies.

Treat your generational responsibilities as a series of sprints rather than a marathon. Marathons may be a great experience if you train for them. When it comes to dealing with these generational tugs, it is helpful to plan things in the short term. This is easier on those supporting others than imagining that this is what life will be for the next five, ten, or twenty years.

Parental health can be something that changes very quickly. Those developments might mean a change in what care is required. At some point, your parent may move into a different circle of care.

Children of boomers may eventually find their niche where the combination of an improved economy, an accumulation of work experience, and the desire to room with friends rather than live at home moves them on. One job offer can change the game for them and for you. Visualizing your children living with you until they are fifty will not help you or them. Instead, having a positive attitude with them as they endure the challenges will give them important support as they endure the disappointments of their early career. Theirs is not the first generation to grow up in a time of financial stress and disappointment. The parents and grandparents of boomers knew about the challenges of world wars and the Great Depression. Those who come from challenging areas of the world today have lived this for many generations. The pre-millennial experience of North American boomers where life always fell into place is more an anomaly than typical. Keep thinking sprints.

The other concept that is helpful is to establish boundaries. Trying to balance the obligations you have to your spouse as well as parents and children requires you to make some choices. Some parents and some children will take anything and everything that they can to get through their challenging times. You and your spouse must think through what you are prepared to do for aging parents and still-dependent children. If you are like most people, you will not be able to do it all.

Set the boundaries with each generation by choosing to do what you can do for the next sprint. Where your resources of time and money do not allow you to do everything that might be needed, look for solutions that involve others. That might mean additional support services for a parent who wants to remain independent.

It could be requiring the boomeranged child to not only work where they can but to do things to support the workload in the home. It can be very helpful for them to volunteer their under-employed time in community service as being busy can keep their skills fresh and their sense of self more positive.

With each generation, review the boundaries in a way that expresses your love and commitment to them but also makes clear the limits of what you can do. That can be very difficult in many family systems where parents or children have learned how to persuade others to do what they want.

A final important concept is to make the decisions of what you are willing to do not on what is being asked and by whom but by who you are. If you can decide to help based on, "I will do this because that is who I am," then you will find it easier to say yes and no to the demands of others.

Ultimately, whatever this tug of war chapter in your story requires, you not only want to get through it – you want to be able to own it. That can happen if you try to keep your sense of integrity where you are acting in a way that is consistent with your values as you do your best to serve the generation that went before and the generation that follows.

THEY WEREN'T KIDDING AFTER ALL

"If you haven't got your health…"

During our carefree time of youth, we ignore the choices that will help us feel better and live longer as we naturally live in the moment. While it would be great to reset our clocks to the teenage years (and before) to modify our diet and exercise patterns, it is always a good decision to be healthy today. We cannot change the past, but we can change our future outlook by making the best choices now.

Poor health impacts all aspects of our life – especially as we get older. Good health is to be valued and is something to be chosen on a daily basis. Our mental and physical health determines so many aspects of our current and future life. As we all age, our health naturally declines. We are more vulnerable to disease and injury as our body systems age from years of function. For some, it can be the onset of chronic pain associated with joints that have worn out from accumulated injuries. Other risks are associated with our vital organs like our heart. Brain function may be inhibited, leading to dementia. Some of us have genetic predispositions that will appear over time.

The best antidote to the aging process is to be healthy. A healthy lifestyle and diet will postpone many chronic diseases that are made worse through poor nutrition and lack of exercise.

How do we stay healthy? Exercising at least three times a week for 30 minutes is beneficial for both physical and mental health (it is important to exercise within the limits and on the advice of your physician based on your current health status). This may include walking with a friend for 30 minutes three times a week. It may be more intensive stretching, aerobics, and weight training. Some tend to not exercise unless they scheduled the time and are accountable to do it – as with a personal trainer. It is not natural for many people to exercise since only a few generations ago, we exercised to live in an agrarian or industrial setting where most people did physical labor to survive.

Our diet is so important to maintaining good health. The daily habit of eating vegetables, fruits, and proteins is important. Taking multi-vitamins and multi-minerals is also helpful. As we age, we need to be intentional in drinking plenty of water each day. Avoid drinking soda pop. Monitor your intake of caffeine. Caffeine after noon can affect that all-important good night's sleep. Moderate the intake of alcohol. Alcohol is a central nervous system depressant and can lead to fatigue that may also disrupt our normal sleep patterns.

Getting plenty of rest is important. It is important to try to allow for eight hours of sleep at night. As we age, our perceived need for sleep is often less than the time that we should sleep. This makes it more difficult to sleep long enough as we age. It is also important not to exercise heavily later in the day. Avoid a heavy meal before bedtime as this also affects the quality of our sleep.

Many avoid going to their doctor as they age out of a fear of learning that something is wrong. Regular check-ups and ongoing treatment of conditions that do appear will make a big difference in how well we age. Many diseases have new and improved treatments over the last generation that will give you a renewed life even as you deal with the disease.

Keep your mind active. Doing a variety of challenges each week benefits our brain health. Playing cards, board games, crosswords, online games, jig-saw puzzles, reading books, listening to music, painting, gardening and similar activities stimulates and exercises our brain. Some websites like Luminosity are designed to keep us mentally active through puzzles and challenges. These all help keep us mentally fit.

Once again, the basics include exercise, plenty of rest, and balanced nutrition. If you want a long life, choose a healthy life; not only are you more likely to live longer, you will enjoy it much more.

GOLDEN SUNSETS OR LOW WINTER SUN

O ne of the decisions many retirees face is whether to stay where they are or move to a warmer climate. Surviving the winters in a northern city can be a badge of honor or the basis for the question, "Why?" The winter break destinations of Florida or Arizona become a year-round destination for many people as they retire. Their change of place is to leave the heat in the summer to return to the more temperate summers in the northern places like Michigan and New England or back home, wherever that might have been. Others prefer to continue in the familiar weather of their home. They like the change of seasons that have accompanied them over their many years. They recognize that each region has its challenges in both weather and living.

A retirement move might help some realize capital from the family home as they downsize. In addition to reducing the size of their home, changing location may also mean moving to a less expensive region of the country. This can stretch retirement dollars over the years.

Beyond the pleasures of warm weather or the savings of moving to an affordable region of the country, other pieces of the puzzle need to be considered.

By moving away, you reduce the number of social contacts that you might have accumulated over your working life. These can include family, friends, neighbors, members of your faith community, and clubs. While it is true that you can always keep in touch and come back to visit, a move does create a break in those relationships.

If you as an individual or as a couple find it easy to create new relationships, you might find it easy to connect with new people in your place of choice. This can be especially true if you move to a community of others who have chosen to live as retirees in search of the golden sunsets for their retirement years.

For those who find it difficult to meet and make new friends, you may find the move is a relief from the tough weather but a challenge in your social world. Finding people and places to make connections will help your sense of well being. It is wise not to create a social life that is totally dependent on a spouse as that can create many stresses on top of the challenges of the retirement years. You need to have a circle of friends and acquaintances, too.

If you choose the low winter sun of your northern climate, recognize that the aging process and cold weather create some challenges of their own. Learning to stay home in storms and leaving the snow-shoveling to others are just some of the many decisions that must be made (and kept) if you are going to live with old man winter.

For those of you who have family in your community, moving south or moving to a less expensive market can reduce the number of contacts you might have with those children and potentially grandchildren. You may not realize how much you might miss the routine contacts that might not seem significant at the time. Many younger family members do move around in search of opportunities for education and jobs, leaving behind the family who is there. So, staying put is no guarantee of proximity to family. Some of your great friends may choose to move. To discover how living at a distance might impact your relationships, you may want to try taking some longer times away in the winter. You can then evaluate how it affects you and your family before you decide to make the big move.

Like many choices in life, you (and your partner) may have to think it through carefully to decide what is most important to you in this season of your life.

Will it be a warm, golden sunset or a low winter sun over the place you will call home?

OLDER & WISER

One of the gifts of growing older is our ability to have perspective on the moments in life that used to strike us with dread or wild enthusiasm. We learn that what seemed like the greatest thing ever may not be as important as we once thought. We also recognize that our mistakes fit the fact that we are human. In our youth, we are superhuman – or so we thought. Over time, we see the other realities of the human condition and learn to accept that as OK too.

How do we deal with our mistakes – great and small – from the past? There are many answers to that question that often involve denying or hiding our failures. The little voices persist in reminding us of "the might have beens": if only we have been better, smarter, surer, or purer in the past. What do you do with your past mistakes?

In the Star Trek movie "The Final Frontier", Captain Kirk confronts the opportunity to be released from his past mistakes by Spock's brother, Sybok. Others in the crew had taken up the offer to be released from their deepest pain and regret – often something unknown to even their closest friends.

Spock was invited by his brother to revisit a memory of rejection by their father, Sarek, because Spock appeared so human and not as Vulcan as Sarek had hoped. Spock told his brother that he was no longer the little boy that Sybok had known so long ago. He had matured beyond that pain. He did not need Sarek's intervention.

For Kirk, now many years into his life and career, there was a different reason to reject the offer of tranquility. He said that, "...pain and guilt can't be taken away with a wave of a magic wand. They're the things we carry with us, the things that make us who we are. If we lose them, we lose ourselves. I don't want my pain taken away! I need my pain!"

As we become older and wiser, we begin to come to terms with the realities of human frailty. We are a combination of our greatest moments and our worst. Some lives are lived with a steady drumbeat – never straying too far up or down. Others are lives lived large – for better and for worse.

Perhaps more than other generations, baby boomers have sought to insulate themselves from negative feelings like pain and regret. In a generation that in its youth was wildly optimistic about changing the world, it has lived the reality that a generation later, the human condition has not changed all that much.

How do you deal with the disappointments and failures that are as much a part of your story as the delights and successes you have experienced?

Kirk acknowledged the pain and guilt that he felt over some of the choices in his past. It is a healthy thing to be able to admit to yourself that you have failed yourself and others along the way, where that is the case. Choices that put ourselves first over the needs of others often bring us pain and disappointment. It reminds us that life and choices do matter. If you could never make a wrong decision or if nothing you chose to do could ever go wrong, you might soon conclude that your choices were not real choices after all.

It is our ability to choose that defines us as human beings. This is not to suggest that we should not strive to do and be our best selves. But if our failures disqualify us from the game of life, we limit the resources for good that each person can contribute by disqualifying those who do not measure up to a perfect standard. To admit that we are only human, acknowledge our mistakes, and move on is healthy. Understanding that failure is part of the human experience is one of the benefits of growing older.

A great theme in faith and literature is redemption. This includes the acknowledgment of failure, but it does not stop there. Redemption takes the fallen person and lifts them up to go on as a better person because they have endured the pain of defeat. The redeemed person has a different strength and humility unknown to the person who has yet to fail or who ignores their poor choices.

So, what do you do with the ups and downs of your life so far? Acknowledge them for what they are. Do not let them keep you down. Instead, use them to motivate you to make a difference in your years ahead.

FEATHERS, FINS, AND FUR

If you have grown up with pets, you will have many memories of the different experiences that they gave you. Some pets were sentimental friends who were there to play along with you and share in your adventures. Others were an exploration of life as you brought home the puppy or kitten so full of energy and mischief. You (or at least your parents) endured the challenges of training the pet and forgiving the chewed shoes or furniture. The hamster or bird eventually grew comfortable with your touch and care. Depending on you and your pet, you bonded to some level of connection that you might now remember.

For some, it was a goldfish in the classic fish bowl. Maybe you are old enough to have had a turtle that lived in one of those 1960s clear plastic containers with a small pool with water and a ramp to climb up with a small green plastic palm tree at the top. Did you have an aquarium filled with a variety of fish?

Most people have pleasant memories of the pets that journeyed along with them in childhood. Pets taught us responsibility as we cared for them. We learned that too much of a good thing – even food – could make them sick. We met the veterinarian and learned about animal health. Sadly, it was often one of our first encounters with loss when we would return home to find the goldfish floating upside down or were told that our pet was too sick or too old to keep any longer. That separation and loss was painful for us.

As life went on, you may or may not have had pets between your teen years and being settled in your adult life. If you had children, you may have included pets as part of their story too. As an adult, you begin to appreciate some of the many things that our parents did for us. Pets bring us full circle in a hurry.

Even the most committed pet owners who may have a series of dogs, cats, budgies, or fish start to look at replacing pets that depart more and more reluctantly. For some people, it is the vision of increased travel that makes the idea of a pet in retirement a burden. For others, the pain of taking that wonderful but sick friend to the vet to say goodbye becomes an experience you do not want to have to do again. We all understand that the beginning of a relationship with a pet also starts the clock running until at some point we will say goodbye. Some fear that if they outlive their pet, their pet will be abandoned. Many people as they approach retirement decide that the pet they have will be their last.

You are probably familiar with the practice of bringing pets – especially dogs – into retirement homes and long-term care facilities. These visitors are very popular with many of the residents who experience the magic that pets can bring into our lives at any age and stage.

It is not just those in long-term care who can enjoy pets. Most people in retirement and through their later years benefit from having a pet. What pet is appropriate for you depends on your pet preferences, finances, and accommodations.

To varying degrees, pets provide us with companionship. Mammals like dogs and cats are especially good at paying attention to us. For those of us who are dog lovers, we enjoy the fact that dogs live very much "in the now" with us. Regardless of whether we have been gone all day or just took out the garbage, the canine friends burst into celebration with tail wagging and eyes fixed on our arrival. They celebrate us without regard to our resume, social standing, or financial success. They practice something that humans rarely achieve with each other – unconditional positive regard. The transference of that enthusiastic response makes us feel good. The bonding that takes place as we pat our dog or cat creates an enhanced sense of well-being no matter how our life is going.

For bird lovers, the chirps and songs of the parakeet or canary are bright and cheerful. Those who enjoy an aquarium or gold fish can watch the movement and interactions of the creatures with their environment.

It is both a blessing and a curse in retirement that we have a loss of routine. The structured rhythm of the work day is no longer there. Many people expand their social routines to engage with others. Some take up a hobby, sports, or a new area of study. Unfortunately, others replace work with time in front of the television.

Routines are a positive part of good mental health and well-being. Establishing those routines (even as they may change along the way) is helpful as we transition into retirement and beyond. Having a pet adds a routine to our life. As our parents were quick to remind us, having a pet is a responsibility. While being finished with our working life and therefore free to do whatever we want sounds appealing, it is part of our human make-up to need to be needed. Responsibilities and routines remind us that we are needed and valuable as persons who make contributions to others.

You have probably met family members or others who drifted through retirement without any sense of purpose or connection. Part of this is due to a breakdown of a sense of being needed. When we have a pet, it gives us a routine to add to whatever else is in our life.

The greatest value of a pet for the retiree is the companionship and affection that pet owners experience. Like many choices we make entering and living past our retirement years, we have to plan ahead. Those entering retirement in committed relationships may not see the need for the companionship of a pet. But if you or your spouse lose the other, it is not a time at which one feels like getting a pet. However, if you already have a pet, they will journey with as you go through the grieving process. That pet will continue to be a bridge to that other person who also shared a life with them and you.

So, whether you prefer feathers, fins, or fur, think about having a pet in your retirement future. They will help you finish well!

A SINGLE FOCUS

Many people enter their retirement years as a single person. For some, this is nothing new as they have been single all their lives. For others, it might be the death of a spouse or the end of a marriage that has changed their status. The years after a career create new opportunities but also include some extra challenges.

For the single person who celebrates their choice to be independent, the retirement years create a new level of freedom to explore their world. Like others who retire, the single person can begin to choose more of how their time is spent, what interests to pursue, and what relationships they wish to nurture.

If you are one of those who did not choose to be single, losing contacts at the workplace can accelerate your sense of loss of that spousal relationship. Many people find the workplace helps them with continuity during a period of loss brought on by a death or divorce. It does not fill the hours after work or overnight, but at least the routines of the day continue along.

There is an important distinction between being alone and being lonely. As people who are in troubled relationships will tell you, you can feel lonely with many people all around you. Many who are solitary by nature or preference enjoy the opportunity to be alone. To be alone can be the best of times.

We all do well to have some time alone. In a fast-paced world, we seldom take the time to pause, much less to pray, meditate, or otherwise reflect on our lives. It actually can give us social energy when we have made the investment in ourselves to be alone.

Being lonely is another matter. While we can all experience the feeling when we are separated from loved ones and friends, it is a destructive feeling if it lasts for a long time.

For those who are unhappy in their singleness, it is good to seek both social and family occasions to engage with others. Many who find themselves single again do not have the confidence to be out with others or to create new relationships. Perhaps they saw themselves as part of a couple only and find that others in their social circle were also part of committed relationships. They might find the presence of a newly single person challenging or uncomfortable. Singles need to find those people who are accepting of their relationship status and supportive of their desire to be in community together.

Social relationships serve many purposes beyond the benefits that they brings to others and to the community. Participating in community with others is also healthy for us.

Single people need to be intentional about their relationships. When you are in a spousal or family relationship, there is a great deal of interaction through the course of life together. People who are on their own and retired may find that days go by between their times with friends and family.

Some of the greatest people who impact their community and their generation are singles who have decided to make a difference.

So, if you are a happily single or a single again, do not forget the family and friends who would like you to connect as well.

Good Morning, Good Morning!

"Good Morning, Good Morning!" may have been a cheery show tune you grew up hearing sung by a mother who wanted to get you up for school. It was one of the many great songs from "Singin' in the Rain": the voices of Debbie Reynolds, Donald O'Connor and Gene Kelly combined to create an optimistic sound typical of the 1950s. The relief of having World War II a few years in the rear-view mirror meant that America was looking forward to better years ahead. Families expressed their confidence in the future by having kids – lots of them. It was the baby boom, and so began a generation that would dominate the attention of generations behind it and the ones that would follow.

This great bulge in the population would concentrate governments, business, and communities on this wave of children as they grew up in the 1950s and 1960s. Advertising, entertainment, and the culture would be swayed by the gravitational force of this generation. Older generations were complicit in and contented with much of this attention. The boomers represented the future. The hopes and dreams of families who knew the Great Depression and World Wars wanted their children and grandchildren to know a better life than they had known. Many families had emigrated from the old world, and North America seemed ready to offer its abundance to a generation who were ready to consume it. The space race, muscle cars, cheap oil, interstate highways, and plastics were a new normal. Advances in technology, a growing middle class, and social progress added to the sense that it would become the best of times.

Reminders of an uncertain and dangerous world were always there too. "Duck and cover" drills announced the Cold War was a threat. Assassinations of John and Robert Kennedy and Martin Luther King interrupted the dreams that each represented. Vietnam, campus unrest, race riots, and Yuppies suggested utopia had not yet been achieved. So much culminated in 1968 that the year was correctly described by ABC News as a "Crack in Time."

Depending on what end of the boom you were born in, you could have a very different perspective on it and life. Those who were born near the end of the boom saw some of the excesses of the early boomers but also benefited from the struggles already achieved. When it came to employment, the early boomers enjoyed the opportunities of a dynamic and innovative economy while the later boomers found it more difficult in a "post-world" – post-Vietnam, post-oil shock, and post-Watergate.

Now, that wave is passing the traditional thresholds of retirement and beyond. Their numbers will continue to tilt the focus and resources of society from the young and middle-aged to an aging population with high expectations for what remains of life. The math of the social contracts created when the boomers were employed does not work with fewer workers left in the generations that follow. The cost of health care and support for seniors means that new strains will not just appear in the budgets of government but between the generations. Limited resources force tough choices. Governments and companies that promised their retirees generous and increasing pensions may find it impossible to continue to meet those commitments. Changing patterns of worldwide wealth and growth no longer guarantee that the jobs and opportunities will always be centered in North America.

Lobby groups for seniors fight any attempt to raise the age of retirement or to adjust benefits in retirement. The harsh realities of bankrupt companies and cities who can no longer afford their legacy costs will force changes that politicians have been unwilling to make in the highly charged "third rail" of politics.

It was a generation to whom much was given.

Individual baby boomers and the generation as a whole will face tough choices. Will the boomers be willing to endure the constraints of living with less? Will they forgo what they expected to receive so that the coming generations might have a better future? Or will boomers feel entitled to everything they expected and resist any changes that do not benefit them?

How boomers choose to balance these issues may do as much to define the legacy of their generation as anything else that has happened in the great wave that changed the world.

ONCE UPON A TIME

Great fishing tales are about the moment of landing the big fish in the boat. But the best fishing tales are always about the one that got away. It is human nature to exaggerate the opportunities missed – especially when we were sure that they were on the line and so very close to landing in our boat.

Growing older includes a number of activities in life that we can no longer do as well, if at all. Changes in our physiology determine that we have peak years when we can do certain activities best. Our strength, stamina, recovery rate, and mental focus all change as we get older. Some sports favor the teens and early twenties. Others reward the mature strength of the later twenties and thirties. Rarely does a sport reward being in your forties or fifties as the optimum age.

If you were someone who enjoyed sports, you know that for a while, you can trade off some speed with experience. The ability to anticipate and be confident in your actions may be more valuable than the tenths of seconds of difference in speed against a younger competitor. However, sooner or later, you lose more that just a step, and you have to start making adjustments. Starting pitchers add new types of pitches to compensate for the reduced speed on their fastball. Then, starters become relievers. The finisher might give you one or two innings of intense pitching, but that is all.

How long you can play is a combination of genetics, training, and injuries. Sooner or later, you have to hang up the cleats unless your sport allows for reduced competition for older players like golf or swimming.

Looking at pictures snapped over a lifetime, we can see many changes. Like the funhouse mirror at a carnival, we look at the image of ourselves in the mirror that is changed and altered by time. Some of the body is larger. Other parts appear drawn. Hair disappears from some places and appears anew in others areas. Colors fade or begin to share space with gray and white. "Puffy" aptly describes the place under the eyes. We look out through the eyes of an eighteen-year-old only to see in the mirror someone more like our parent or grandparent. It can be quite a shock even as we watch it happen.

Over a lifetime, racing becomes running. Running becomes jogging. Jogging becomes walking. The walks become slower and shorter. Eventually, a cane or a walker might be our companion.

We live between the two worlds of resistance and acceptance. Aging is something we wish to resist. We do not want to concede things that we like to do. We especially do not want to give up those things that we like to do well. At all costs, we will try to postpone the physical changes that aging can bring. Somewhere in each of these battles, we start to move toward acceptation. We gradually accept that we will never be as fast as we once were. Like youth itself, time tests and takes from us some of those abilities that were only available for a season.

In its place, life offers us other strengths. These are powers that are not physical but social, mental, and financial. While these gains are not in a straight line, we usually find ourselves stronger in these areas over the decades. Much of this is gained from experience. We often associate the word seniority with the workplace. In fact, it can also be applied to life in general.

The process of aging has been especially painful for the baby boomer generation. Unlike many previous generations who enjoyed their youth while looking forward to growing older, boomers have embraced the idea of "age is hereby postponed until further notice."

When signs of aging and the changes that it creates confront the boomers, they often respond in disbelief. How can this be? I cannot be getting old – my parents and grandparents were old. Through improved nutrition, exercise, and medical care, we have been told that we can expect to take 10 years off our age. Thus, 50 is the new 40 and 70 is the new 55. The feelings of invincibility so naïve and yet helpful in our youth can lead to painful consequences when we try to do everything now that we did then.

Healthier is an attitude that embraces aging well rather than pretending that we are immune from life's clock. Extending our best into the future in all areas of life is good. Ignoring the compensations life offers for those who gradually lose the joys of a young body is to miss out on the opportunities we have been given for each age and stage of life.

Get baby boomers talking about all they once did in their youth. You will think you are gathered around a campfire, hearing the glowing tales of an old fisherman about the one that got away. It is always polite to smile, nod in approval, and say, "That's amazing!"

PROFITS AND LOSSES

Life is a series of gains and losses. So much is gained in our earliest years of development. Change is rapid, and we continue to add to our knowledge, abilities, and relationships in the decades of our life. Over that same time, we also experience grief and loss. Grief and loss may or may not be interchangeable depending on our response to loss.

By the third act of our lives, we face a significant amount of loss. We tend to lose some or all of our freedom in our health, mobility, and even finances. In the natural cycle of life, it is more than likely that we will outlive our parents and perhaps siblings and friends, even our spouse, partner, or significant others. How we respond to these losses in the psychologist Erik Erikson's life stage of generativity is a fairly accurate predictor of how we will enter the last of these stages of social development. Will it be seeing life with integrity or despair?

As noted in earlier chapters, it is important as you go through middle age to offer something to the generation that will come behind you. Many times, this is through children; however, with those who do not have children, it might be through extended family, the professions that we engage in, or perhaps by investing in younger members of a group such as a church or club. There is an innate desire as individuals reach their 40s, 50s, and 60s to try to improve the futures of the individuals who will come after.

One of the biggest losses medically can include our walking ability. We may have to ambulate with assistance, a walker, or even a wheelchair. We may get to the point where it is not safe for us to drive our car or travel independently. In response, we can use optimism and humor as a defense mechanism, or we can choose to be bitter, angry, and ultimately depressed.

How we handle this important phase of life ultimately determines much of how we will be remembered. Our third act can create a lasting impression that can overshadow the first and second acts of our story. Included in this is how we deal with loss and grief as we age.

What can you do?

Establish a support system as you age. For many, there is a support system built-in with their families. Their life network often includes spouses, children, pets, co-workers, and friends at church, all of whom may include us as well. That interconnectivity offers support to each member – including the older ones in the group. Sometimes, we have neighbors who can be a part of our support system.

Our networks change significantly as we age. This is most dramatic after the loss of our parents, close family members, and old friends as well as the increasing limitations on our physical freedom. New supports may be introduced to address our particular needs. Physically, that might be someone to aid us with daily routines. Just as important, we need to ensure that we have good social support. This is another example where choices to connect with others in our younger, active years pay dividends as we age.

All of us will deal with grief and loss over our lifetime. Some of us respond by erecting a façade with a solid exterior when deep down we are really hurting. Others tend to be more emotional or perhaps dramatic in expressing their feelings. Whatever type of person you tend to be, it is important to reconcile how you deal with grief and loss. When choosing isolation to deal with loss with a stiff upper lip, we benefit from allowing others to come alongside during difficult periods in life. No one is immune from grief and loss; it is a shared human experience. Supportive counseling from a mental health professional or perhaps a clergy member or seeking the support of a close friend might also help us move forward when we feel like everything has stopped. Sometimes, we might even need medications to help us cope with difficult times of grief and loss.

It is important to not ignore your feelings as well as your limitations as you get older. There are those out here that are able and willing to help.

Identify and build those resources now to help you make the third act a profitable time of life even as you experience the inevitable losses that will occur.

NEXT TO THE GREATEST GENERATION

A long shadow has always been cast over the baby boomer generation. They follow what has been coined by Tom Brokaw as, "The Greatest Generation" of men and women who were children of the Great Depression and who fought in World War II.

As is true with any sweeping generalizations about people of a time, the generation before the boomers was full of greatness and weaknesses too.

The older generation stood for challenges met, responsibilities kept, courage shown, and humility in victory. The quintessential exemplar from this generation was a quiet man who grew up under difficult conditions on a Midwest farm or in a poor part of a large city. While the Great Depression continued, he was called upon to defend the homeland and fight for freedom abroad. Doing his duty, he followed orders, toughed it out, and persisted until the wars in Europe and Asia were over. Surprisingly durable and tough for men from a free people, they took on the highly structured and disciplined soldiers from nations with fanatical visions of their destiny. The American and Canadian soldiers, along with the other Allies, fought the good fight and celebrated the victory.

Returning home to their grateful nations, the vets quickly reintegrated into the life of post-war Canada and the United States. They returned to the farms, shops, and factories in support of a newly revived economy. Along with the men, women of that generation stepped out of their traditional roles as members of the war effort running farms, working in factories, and doing many jobs only recently filled exclusively by men. They had changed the outcome of the war and the wartime had in turn changed them.

The growing momentum of the economy led to better times and the hopefulness of the 1950s and 1960s. Opportunities for reward and progress in exchange for a hard days work became a social contract that brought stability and prosperity to that generation and the many children they added – the baby boomers.

The baby boomers were unlikely to replicate the successes of the generation that parented them. Born in good times, they did not know the deprivation and struggle of the Great Depression. The wars that they grew up knowing were the Korean War and the infamous Vietnam War. The boomers did not experience the hard times that shaped their parents, leading the younger generation to a sense of entitlement and self-indulgence. The natural pushback against the previous generation led to the boomers to reject much of what they saw as mechanical obedience to tradition and the acquisition of wealth. To the parents of boomers, they despaired at the sight of so many tuning out the core values that the parents believed were responsible for gains made during their lifetime and the generation before. As the Vietnam War worsened over its decade of growth, opposition to the war blurred the distinction between soldier and war. Soldiers were despised or forgotten by many when they returned home. It was not their father's war.

Of course, the greatest generation was not the perfect generation. The same stoic silence about their war years that was celebrated did not lead to easy communication with their children. As much as it was a difference in styles, tastes, and priorities, the generation gap was largely a communication gap.

As we now look back on it, many of these men and women carried the suffering of the Great Depression and the war bottled up inside them. The cultural taboo of talking about those days (outside of a VFW or legion hall) meant that this was a burden often carried alone. What we now call PTSD (post-traumatic stress disorder) did not first appear with the war in Iraq or Afghanistan. Unnamed, it was present in veterans of all wars. Unwillingness or inability to share their war stories meant that this condition would fester in the hearts and minds of these men for the rest of their lives. As with veterans today, it was a legacy of war that led to alcoholism, drug abuse, depression, and even suicide.

It was not until the baby boom generation that many of the social challenges of society were addressed. The stability of the greatest generation also meant that there was little room for change or progress. Life was largely accepted as it was.

So, as the baby boomers have grown up and now look back on their generation, it is a good thing to continue to tip our hats to the generation that went before. They deserve it. But baby boomers have contributed to a better society as well. In the end, most of the greatest generation looked past the quirks and craziness of their children. They loved the generations that followed and wished them well. If you look closely, you might see a bit of a shadow from our generation over the next. That tends to be the way of the world no matter what the generation is called.

SCROOGE & SAWYER

Ebenezer Scrooge and Tom Sawyer are characters in stories set a century apart and an ocean away from each other. One is the tale of an old man at the spent end of his life while the other is of a young boy full of vim and vigor. However, Charles Dickens and Mark Twain included one common scene in these very different tales. The effect on each was life-changing but in very different ways.

Ebenezer and Tom each saw their own funerals.

For Scrooge, the third of the spirits who visited him on that Christmas Eve took him to see the time when he would be absent from his usual place. Afterwards, Scrooge saw some acquaintances signing the book of remembrance with derisive comments about the life he had lived. The undertaker and servants were dividing the spoils from his person and his home. No one mourned his passing. Finally, he saw his grave with his named etched on the tombstone.

Tom, along with friends Huckleberry Finn and Joe Harper, had ventured off to an island where they were playing pirates. Away too long, the town folk assumed that they had all drowned. The boys hid as they watched the men sounding the river in search of their bodies. The lads now feared that they were in great trouble and feared the consequences for the disappearing. A funeral was planned, and the good people of the town were mourning the loss of these three young lives. After a time of remorse, Tom convinces the others to return with him to the funeral service and surprise everyone with the good news that they were not dead after all. They boys hear at the funeral how much they are missed and see the great distress of the community that was gathered in mourning. The boys were amazed to hear all the generous things said about them.

Then, as planned, they reappeared alive and well, much to the relief and celebration of the congregation.

Have you ever imagined what your funeral service or wake would be like? As you get older, you accumulate many funeral occasions where you hear friends and loved ones recount the life lived. If it was your turn soon, what would those in your life say in remembrance of your time here?

Every day that we have left is an opportunity to make a difference in our world. Growing older, we begin to understand that it is not the grand gestures that people remember; it is the small acts of kindness that touch the people in our story. We all have the possibility of being remembered well, in spite of the painful chapters that are also part of the stories of most people today. Rather than letting the past cause you to despair and give up, be glad that you have a today to make a difference in the world around you. Take the wisdom and experience you have gained to this point in your life and use it to benefit others. Like so much of life, where we give, we receive back much more than we could have imagined.

The boys in Tom Sawyer went from feeling frustration at being too tightly controlled and misunderstood to having a sense of belonging. Those tentative relationships with the good adults in their world now moved forward to a sense of commitment and connection. It did not end the challenges and adventures that would await them in life, but it changed how they saw themselves and their place in the world.

For Scrooge, the awakening after the visit of the spirit of Christmas to come gave him an opportunity for redemption. He realized at last how his life had focused on matters of money instead of being in the real business of life, serving others. Ebenezer began to set right the relationships that were ignored or damaged. He finally understood that Christmas was not a "humbug" – a trick or deception, in the parlance of the day – but something genuine and healing. Scrooge took the time he had left and invested it in the people of his world. Family connections were restored and employees were fairly compensated, and he became "uncle" to the disadvantaged Tiny Tim. Not only did Ebenezer keep Christmas but it was said that Christmas was in his heart. It was also said that he was "Better than his word" in the years that remained.

Scrooge could have looked at the years and opportunities lost and concluded he was beyond hope. Instead, he decided to finish well. He was determined to make a difference in his world with the time that he had left. He was finally free to know the love and joy that life had offered him in the past, if only he could have looked beyond the trials of the human experience. Ebenezer Scrooge stands as a beacon of light for each person to answer the question, "What will you do with the time that remains?" Scrooge saw his death and chose life.

Do not abandon hope for the rest of your story. How will you use the time you have left?

PREDICTING THE WEATHER

In the movies, the old-timer can tell the young whippersnapper that it is going to rain. They can either feel it in their bones or their bunion is acting up. It seems like a strange concept until you get a bit older yourself. That spot where you had a broken bone or where there is a touch of arthritis suddenly does seem to speak out when the bad weather is coming on.

For many of us, the pain does not just come along when a low pressure front is moving into the area. We might have chronic pain that nags at us every day. These might be physical or emotional aches from the accumulated injuries of life. This can have a huge emotional impact on your daily life along with those family and friends in your world.

Why we have pain in our lives is a topic for philosophical and theological debate. One of our favorite authors, C.S. Lewis, has written an entire book entitled "The Problem of Pain," in which he addresses the debate that occurs within us.

There are different types of physical pain that increase with age. Arthritis is a chronic progressive illness that affects your bones and joints. Another more common type of progressive pain is fibromyalgia, in which the actual nerves cause pain to individuals. Whether it is sharp or dull aches or pains, many of us will experience some type of pain as we age. Also associated with aging are chronic headaches. For others, it is back or leg pain or pain in the fingers.

There are millions of individuals out there who struggle with pain on a daily basis. Dealing with physical pain can result in additional emotional pain. As one goes through their 40s, 50s, and 60s, how they deal with physical and emotional pain is an important part of the third act.

There are many options in the treatment of chronic pain that include medicines; warm or hot baths, Jacuzzis, or steam; massage therapy with myofascial release; topical creams; acupuncture, and chiropractic care. Many new and innovative solutions are being researched and created since we have an aging population, and pain is a big factor in quality of life. Consult your healthcare professionals to find the combination of treatment solutions that is best for your particular challenges.

Many people do not realize that a variety of the antidepressants prescribed for depression are also beneficial in pain control. The reason is that there is a chemical that translates pain in our nervous system that translates into mood as well. There is a close correlation between antidepressant medications and the added benefit of the healing properties for physical pain that these medications can provide. This is not a new phenomenon but has been evolving.

Of course, all of us want to totally alleviate pain in our lives. When we are unable to eliminate pain (physical or emotional) in our lives, we need to look at options for treatments and maintenance that will help us as we process the pain.

Experiencing physical pain on a day-to-day basis wears us down. It can lead to some fairly significant mood disorders. It is important to take care of yourself and to not ignore your chronic pain. Make sure that you have had a medical evaluation to determine the cause of pain and different treatment alternatives. Today, there are even physicians that specialize in pain treatments that can be very helpful. Many medications that are available today to treat pain are non-addictive and quite helpful. There are other options today besides narcotics for the long-term treatment of pain. It is important to utilize support systems and augmentation therapies as well as mainstream medical support. The treatment of pain is multidimensional and multi-factorial. There is not just one pill or one pathway that treats all types of pain. Do not neglect the emotional pain that might develop for you or a loved one as a result of dealing with chronic pain issues.

In summary, there are resources out there to help those who struggle with pain on a daily basis, whether it is physical and/or emotional. Do not isolate yourself, and let others help you as they are able. While no one fully understands another's pain, those who have experienced pain and loss are often able to encourage and comfort those who are going through the same experience. That can be something good coming from a challenge in your life.

Oh, and do not be surprised if you become more reliable than the complex weather forecasting computer models as you feel that next low front coming your way.

WHAT'S LEFT IN YOUR BOX?

Sooner or later, you or one of your siblings will have "the box" passed on to you. It might be a single box or a series of storage containers. As you open it, you will find some of the mementos of family life that have now been passed along to your care. With the death of a grandparent, other relative, and eventually your parents, it will someday be yours to open.

Inside, you will find echoes of their life and perhaps other things passed down to them. Often there are photographs, letters, newspaper clippings, or a ring, necklace, or other personal item that they treasured. Some may have real value, like a coin collection or stamp album. Family heirlooms that have been passed down through the generations may be there. Legal documents like birth certificates, marriage licenses, or passports might officially announce what was part of their story.

Some things were clearly not so significant to the rest of the world. A favorite pocket knife, special books worn through many readings, a tie clasp, a family Bible, or a pocket watch all point to elements of a life's routine. These were some of the things that mattered to the person who included them in their box of memories.

These are things that survived the many moves and the resulting toss of things not used for a while. They were not lost in the fires, thefts, or accidents of life along the way. If they are from previous generations, they also survived the evaluation of the descendents who looked at them and kept them to pass along. It is amazing how many things that are valued by one person or one generation do not connect with someone else.

Of course, some ancestors mistakenly assumed that descendants would like the equivalent of the number of items saved for a presidential library. Why did the Smithsonian never call? Many a storage locker could be filled with the unsorted or hoarded collections of seemingly anything and everything a person ever encountered. But, for most people, it will be a box or two that continues on.

Most of the saved items had some special sentiment attached to them. It might have been the occasion it was received at one of the passages of life like a wedding or retirement. It might have been valued because of who gifted it to the person – a special friend, a teacher, or a valued member of the family.

As you hold an item, a person's face may come to mind. You might be able to visualize that person with it, holding it, using it, treasuring it. As you read the newspaper clipping, it might tell a story you already knew, or it might be news to you. If you are fortunate enough to have had organized ancestors, you might find photographs with the names and dates on the back. Reading a letter to your loved one might give you a window into the times of the life of the friend or relative who wrote to them. If it was correspondence from your loved one, then you can imagine a bit more about them as they described the great and the mundane stories of life recorded in the letter.

It is a strange thing to think of a life of 70 or 80 years being reduced to a few items in a box. To be remembered is the hope of most people down through history. Monuments, tombstones, art, and photographs are just some of the ways people hope to live in memory when their years of life are over.

Of course, what was truly valuable and valued was the person's life. These items are but touchstones of remembrance that give us a physical connection to them. It was the life they lived and the people they touched on their journey that are of lasting value. We all carry the stories of those who went before us though the lives they shaped during their time. It is true in families where the genetics and the decisions of the ancestors live on in their offspring. The ways that they impacted the lives of their friends and community are also part of the heritage passed down. While good ancestors do not guarantee good descendants and are we doomed to repeat any negative choices of our elders, the stories and traits do echo in the generations that follow.

If your time was up this year, what would be left in your box? The memorabilia would be interesting but not as important as what you did to serve the needs of family, friends, and the community.

So, go ahead. Get your memory box organized with names on pictures and explanatory notes for items that may not be obviously important to your descendants. Do not neglect the opportunity to add to your story with the time you have left by making a difference for good in the lives of your circle of family, friends, and beyond. The tradition of being a positive influence in your world is a great legacy to pass along.

CUPID'S ARROWS

Baby boomers may be surprised to find themselves a target for Cupid or wishing to employ his skills to direct an arrow or two on their behalf later in life. For different reasons such as the death of a spouse, divorce, or a falling out in relationships, you may find yourself alone and not in a significant relationship as you enter midlife and beyond.

Many books and movies explore the hopes and fears of new relationships in later life. Could I? Should I? Would it be wise, or will I be the one wearing the hashtag #nofoollikeoldfool?

As was true in our youth, there are many motivations for wanting to enter a committed relationship. Romance, adventure, and sexual fulfillment continue to be important. In later life, the most valued part of the relationship is companionship.

Some people are quite content to not be in a primary relationship. They may have outlived their spouse and prefer that this stage of the journey not include someone else in that place. A painful divorce may make the idea of trusting someone else with your heart not something you wish to do again.

The most important sustaining element of the relationship is the ability to get along well with the other person. That does not mean that the other person has to have identical tastes or interests that we have. Nor do we have to be opposites to compliment the other. Instead, we have to have those elements of a good friendship, a similar direction in life, and an enjoyment of time spent together. The benefits of a primary relationship can look very different to someone in their 50s and beyond compared with those in their 20s and 30s. Many of the passages enjoyed (and survived) by young couples have passed, including building families and careers.

Older individuals understand better that any new relationship has a clock ticking with it as health and life can quickly change. The "sickness and health" clause in the wedding vow does not seem so distant or abstract. The "richer and poorer" clause is also more complicated as there is less time to recover from bad decisions or challenging times. Some worry that the other's interest in them might be mostly for their potential as a solution to care for them financially or physically as age and time take their toll. These people are alone but not so lonely that they wish to try again.

Many do look for and find love later in life. They take on the same risks that the young do but with a new advantage. They have experience and perspective. A lifetime of knowing and recognizing different types of people give the opportunity to sort out more effectively what kind of person will be a great companion for the road ahead. The potential for relationship, intimacy, and joy from a positive relationship outweigh the cautions and risks ever-present in making a commitment to another person. They find added meaning to their life by being a member of "we" rather than "I" alone.

As is true in any relationship, do not seek someone else to fix the issues that are present in your life. Do not imagine that being in a relationship will be the same as returning to your 20s. It is not a secret path to the fountain of youth. Instead, bring your best self to the relationship. Do not see it as a 50/50 proposition. Each one must give 100% to the relationship to make it truly successful and satisfying.

There are those who believe that their true love came and is now gone. They do not wish to consider another to take that special place. Others consider the meaning of the vows "till death do us part" as a reminder that all relationships on earth will end. They consider another relationship to be a possibility.

Loneliness can develop in or outside a relationship at any age. It can be particularly painful in later life when combined with many other typical losses on the journey. Do not expect friends and family members to be able to read your mind if you are lonely. On the other hand, do not let friends and family make assumptions for your need for a relationship later in life. Be vocal and tell them what you need and what you want.

If you want to find a relationship later in life, do not let age stand in the way. Things might be different than when you were in your 20s. You do not have to live someone else's stereotype of romance and relationships in midlife and beyond. Take action steps so that you can be where you want to be during a time of great transition.

Baby boomers, and even those older than baby boomers, can find romance and meaning in the latter stages of life. It is potentially therapeutic to be able to nurture and care for someone other than yourself, no matter what age you are. Pursue your dreams. Pursue needed relationships.

Do not be surprised to hear the odd arrow go whizzing by even if it was a long time since you last saw Cupid smile.

GOOD WILL

Legal decisions need to be made for the probability we all face of infirmity and for the certainty of death. Death is a subject that people avoid as if you can keep death further away by not talking about it. For the sake of your loved ones, take the time to face planning your estate – meaning your instructions for your assets and liabilities after your death.

Many people assume that they do not need to have a will until they are wealthy or advanced in years. It is wise for every adult to have a will. This does not just make the legal issues clearer in the event of your death; it guides your loved ones on what your wishes and directions are.

While it is not required in many jurisdictions to have a lawyer create your will, it is a good idea to do so. Do you know the difference between the words "vague" and "ambiguous" if asked? Words matter. This is especially true when it comes to the law and courts. Vague or ambiguous instructions in a will can force something that should be easy to understand to have to be reviewed in a court to determine what was meant. One of the advantages of using a lawyer who does estate planning as part of his practice is that he has the training and the experience to help you word your instructions clearly. As important is the long list of "what ifs" to consider in case your first ideas no longer apply. A good lawyer will take you through the process so that you can express clearly what you would like to have done with your assets and possessions when you die. It is worth the investment.

One of the functions of creating your will is to appoint an executor(s). This person has the responsibility to carry out your instructions. Often, he or she is a spouse or close family member. Sometimes, she or he is a close friend with business experience who can follow through for you. It is always recommended that you meet with your executor before he or she is appointed in your will to be sure that he or she is willing to serve. You also should go over the instructions with them so that they hear it from you. Normally you have alternative executors to serve if the original one you appointed is unable to serve when needed.

How do you divide your estate? The pain caused by a death can be compounded if a will is not in place or if it is poorly designed. It may also create an opportunity to provide some healing. Sadly, many wills have the opposite effect as they are used to settle scores or to stick the knife into an unfortunate relationship one more time. Harsh words or choices can leave a legacy of pain. Instead, it is wise to try to use the words that will be spoken on your behalf after you are gone to make a positive statement.

If you can, try to treat your children or other relationships as "equitably" as possible. For some, that means an identical percentage of what is left. Sometimes you cannot be "identical" with the assets due to what they are. So, in those cases, be as balanced as you can be so that there is less reason for conflict at the difficult time when they have just lost you.

Living wills and powers of attorney are another topic to discuss with a lawyer. These become the sources of legal guidance for those caring for you if you are incapacitated by accident or illness. It describes your wishes about healthcare and property decisions if you can no longer make them for yourself.

Will yourself to a lawyer to get this organized if you have not done so recently. You will save others additional grief and expense. You will create some good will along the way, too.

IMPROVING YOUR SERVE

One of the characteristics of people who have a great "third act" in life is their willingness to serve others. For some, it is the use of the wealth that they have accumulated over their working years. Others discover the satisfaction that comes from using their business or other leadership experience to help charitable and community groups be more effective in their mission. Many people just enjoy seeing the real-time results of their efforts in building a Habitat for Humanity home, offering homeless people hot meals to enjoy, or being there when a less fortunate family needs a new winter coat and boots for their children.

How can you make a difference in your service of others?

Begin with a servant's heart. This is not something that is reserved for retirement, but it does matter when you are trying to serve others effectively. In its simplest form, it means that I am going to put your best interests above my own. For the time we are serving you, I am going to do my best to make your life better with the resources that I have. This effort must be about whom we serve, not about what we can gain from being altruistic. If our service is about balancing the books of our life, we will have missed the real opportunity that service offers. Our service is focused on the needs of the people we serve. Period. Full stop. Unless we have that sorted out, we are probably not ready to serve others since our mixed motives will cloud our judgment and color our attitude.

Give your best. Times of service are not where we give our leftover selves. In times of service, we give our best efforts. Service is not where we take it down to second gear or neutral and hope that we can just get by through coasting along. Think of what you love to do and the energy you are willing to put into those activities. That is the kind of energy that those we serve deserve as well. This comes from a basic understanding that every person has intrinsic value. Their life experiences, social context growing up, and even whatever terrible choices they might have made do not mean that they are not valuable as people. If we are willing to discriminate against others who are in difficulty, we probably are not the ones who should be serving. The old phrase, "There but by the grace of God go I!" has to be at the root of our service. If we believe that, it could never have happened to us; we have not read enough history or talked to enough people who have been there. It is not only those who are in generational poverty or from the drug culture who can end up in a tragic condition.

Life-changing experiences can take the great and the average people to places they never imagined. Remove the support systems that once were there and many people could quickly slide into poverty and desperation. It is only in our recognition that all human beings are broken and scarred by life that we discover how close any of us are to a very different journey. If you were raised by stable and loving parents with the necessities of life always there, you were given a great gift of possibilities. If you were not, then you will have to struggle hard to break through.

Start with your time. The finite commodity that all of us share is our time. We do not know how many seconds of life we will have over the course of our journey. Get connected with an opportunity that is not just good enough to give your money or advice – get involved with something you would be willing to invest your time in doing. That is a useful test. By all means, give money and lend your expertise, too. But without the willingness to make a commitment of time, you may be in the wrong community or charitable effort.

Let the results take care of themselves. We sometimes expect that service is like Newtonian physics in that every action has an equal and opposite reaction that can be seen. More often, it is like how water changes the land. Over time, water can change the way the land looks as it cuts through soil and rock to find its path. The Grand Canyon was carved by the steady flow of water running along the Colorado River that over time changed everything there. The same is true when we serve. It is that steady flow of effort that can break through the most hardened lives if we commit to being there.

We are never too old or too young to serve others. It is the antidote to many of the poisons of life where greed, envy, pride, and selfishness blind us to the better life that comes in serving others.

So, pick up your racket and ball and start serving.

DO YOU MIND?

There is a trending movement in the mental health field called mindfulness. It is not a new concept as mindfulness goes back to biblical times as well as its infusion in oriental philosophy.

Mindfulness describes the concept that it is important for all of us to live in the moment rather than being consumed by worry and anxiety about things we cannot change. Many of us live in fear about the future. Worry about our finances, health, family, and employment all can crowd our thinking and clutter our mind. When we are able to think more clearly about these issues that bother us, we realize that we have very little that we can do to change many of the things that we worry about.

We should do what we can, of course. If you worry about having poor health in the future, it is important to address your exercise program and your diet now so that you can change your future. If you worry about finances, it is important to address those now with regard to spending patterns and savings programs. These are things that will affect your future. From a biblical perspective, it is stated that we should be anxious for nothing, trusting in God's provision for us. From an oriental philosophy, mindfulness through meditation brings perspective and a happier life.

Mindfulness involves letting go of control and letting go of fear and worry. Mindfulness is a state of mind that has to be practiced and remembered. It is not the norm for most of us living in western society to live in the moment. The business of our life, the business of our jobs, and the fears that we all confront can be managed through mindfulness. Practice living in the moment and do not worry about what you cannot change.

If we focus on living in the moment, then we do not focus on fear of the future or fear of the past. The past is over. We cannot change the past. We cannot change our behaviors in the past. If we need to offer forgiveness towards someone who has harmed us or that we have harmed, then we must do so.

There are individuals who have a harder time practicing mindfulness than others. These individuals include those that are clinically depressed or anxious or have obsessive-compulsive disorder. If we need to seek professional counsel for dealing with mindfulness, we must do so.

The serenity prayer in the Alcoholics Anonymous recovery program focuses on mindfulness in that it asks for wisdom to know the difference between what we can and cannot change. We must change what we can, not live in fear, and accept what we are unable to change.

The foundation of mindfulness can be incorporated into all of our lives in different ways. Living in the moment creates more balance, a serene life, and greater happiness. It is something we need to practice, and like any worthwhile exercise; it will make us stronger and healthier for the days ahead.

CHASING THE DREAM

A favorite destination for many is the state of Florida. The generation of baby boomers has something in common with one of the earliest European visitors to what is now Florida in 1513. That explorer was Juan Ponce de León of Spain.

Ponce de León, it was written, had heard rumors of a land with a magical spring that restored youth. Apparently, he was only in his early forties, but perhaps the hardships of a life at sea, exploring the New World, and the politics of being Governor of Puerto Rico were enough to make him long for the younger years.

He (and we) is not alone in wishing we could turn back the clock. Down through history, the hope of a rediscovered youth has occupied many people. Talk of healing waters goes back to Biblical times in the Jordan and at the pool of Bethesda. Many wish that they could hang on to that youthful appearance and vitality by halting and then reversing the aging process.

Our society is full of anti-aging products and services. It is a big business built on a generation that celebrated its youth when all things were possible. It also feeds on our belief that without looking young, we will no longer be attractive or relevant. Being young means you are happy and successful. If your birth certificate will no longer support the fact of being young, you want to keep up the illusion by whatever means as long as possible.

The message is pervasive on magazine covers, in the movies, on television shows, and in advertising. It makes you wonder how the generations past looked at the baby boomers, who discounted their elders because they were over thirty. Now, with boomers all over 50, our generation wishing to look like those actually in their youth might be ironically appropriate.

Now, the elusive fountain has been replaced with a potion of chemicals, injections, surgeries, and devices that promise a younger-looking you. This obsession distracts many people from living their lives while draining their pocket books. Each surgery creates new issues and imperfections, if only because the result is not how we looked in our mind's eye so long ago.

The antidote to this fruitless chase is to focus on healthy aging and wellness. Having of the ingredients going into being your best, healthy self will be the most reliable anti-aging strategy. Healthy-looking people look younger. Nothing replaces the youthfulness of authentic wellness.

It is no secret that a healthy diet and exercise are two of the key factors in healthy aging and looking well for your age. Large amounts of alcohol will add years to how you look while often adding medical complications and ultimately shortening your life at the same time.

What is the true difference between an unhealthy obsession with looking young versus the better choice of healthy aging? As we all enter our 40s, 50s, 60s, and beyond, it is inevitable that our bodies will age and show those signs of aging that include wrinkles, change in hair color, loss of muscle tone, and perhaps more fatigue. When one is younger, it is common to go overboard with exercise, dieting, makeup, and even plastic surgery to remain looking young. At that time, one is perhaps looking for a spouse or to be accepted in a business organization or social club.

It is unhealthy for someone who is 60 to take the risks and spend the money in the hopes that they will look 20 or 30 again. We have all seen the tragedy of someone who looked healthy only to end up with plastic surgery that distorted their pleasant features.

That is not healthy aging.

This is not a criticism of efforts for us to look our healthy best. The negative crossover point is when it becomes a severe obsession. That is when we need to reevaluate the meaning and purpose of our lives.

We all have some type of minimal conception of our age. Chronologically, we may be 50 or 60, but inside of us, we may still feel like a young adult.

It is important for us to step back and not be sucked into the obsession in our society whose message is that staying and looking young forever means happiness, prosperity, and good health. Age has its own rewards like wisdom, even as it trades us for elements of our youth.

Drink plenty of water daily. This helps maintain good health. Engage in a healthy exercise program on a regular basis. Eat healthy foods. Take your vitamins. Make sure you keep up with your visits to the dentist and the doctor. Be sure to take time for yourself, your family, and your friends. Take time to smell the roses.

Focus on being the best you can be at whatever age you are. People who age well within their souls and relationships radiate a fountain of youth that makes them more attractive than any combination of pills, creams, and scalpels could ever achieve.

MOON RIVER

One of the greatest titles we can have is old friend. The song Moon River, famously sung by Andy Williams and from the movie "Breakfast at Tiffany's", celebrates the journey of life with an old friend. With lyrics by Johnny Mercer and music by Henry Mancini, it pictures two poor friends hoping to cross a great river on their way to see the wide world that awaits. They even hope to find the elusive rainbow's end that might just be around the next bend of the journey with the unstated suggestion of finding wealth after all.

The sentimental song reminds us that, while we may have destinations or achievements in mind throughout life, it is the journey that matters. Included in the story of the journey is who traveled it with us.

Who are the people who have journeyed with you along the years of your life? Who qualifies as your "Huckleberry friend?" For many people, it is a spouse with whom they explored the wide world. Perhaps you have a life-long friend who shared the adventures with you. Maybe it was someone who came along in Act II of your life.

These great friendships often are tested along the way. Moves, other relationships, and growing older can accentuate the differences and stress the relationship. Even the best of friends can disappoint each other with decisions that were badly made. How you move on from those let-downs is not just a predictor of how long your friendship will last but how much you actually value the friendship itself.

Great friends are often not identical in their personalities or even all their interests. What they do share is some chemistry or connection that brings value to the relationship that the other person can recognize and appreciate.

For most people, we need to start our old friendships while we are young. We then have to nurture and grow those friendships over our middle age when a busy life and changing geographies can cause us to neglect those people.

It takes work to keep a friendship going over many years. Shared intense experiences like college or war often generate lifelong friends because of the challenges faced together. There are certain times in our life that we are more likely to make new friends. In our school days, we are often put together with people who are also new to the situation and therefore more open to friendships developing. Similarly, serving in the military demands a level of connection in what is one of the most critically interdependent experiences in life. On a lesser scale of intensity, working at a summer camp or being part of a community or faith group also provides this kind of opportunity to connect.

On the many levels of friendship from acquaintances to best friends, there are different levels of commitment and expectation. Whether two people move toward a closer friendship is always a choice. Will each take the risk of being more open so that a higher level of relationship is possible? If the risk is accepted and the other person risks opening themselves in return, then the friendship will grow. The back and forth between risking and accepting is the key to becoming strong friends.

As time passes, you accumulate shared memories of events and people together. Like the old raft floating down the river, the journey fills up with stories to enjoy later on. "Do you remember?" is a question to be asked of old friends.

If you do not have enough quality friendships, decide to add new friends to your mix. Be intentional. Look at those in your life and choose those people who might become good friends. If you are willing to work on it, friends today might become old friends before you know it. Who would you like as an old friend?

Today is the day to invest in those people we hope will call us "old friend" in the years to come.

TRY TO REMEMBER

As we all age, there will be noted changes in "cognition" or brain functioning. Some of us will personally encounter some type of dementia or have a loved one or friend who will develop it.

A normal brain functions in several different areas that include learning, memory, language, perceptual/motor skills, complex attention, executive functioning, and social cognition. Over time, it is normal to have some progressive forgetfulness. Perhaps we forgot where we placed our keys or our purse. Maybe we forgot a doctor's appointment or a loved one's birthday. It is normal to have some forgetfulness as we get older. There are those for whom forgetfulness increases faster than for others.

What is not normal for the aging individual is a medical illness of the brain called dementia. Dementia is a broad term for all brain illnesses that affect memory, concentration, language skills, and executive function. Everyone will have some level of forgetfulness, but not everyone will develop dementia. Dementia is usually diagnosed where there is a gradual decline in cognitive functioning. There is a noticeable impairment of independence in everyday activities. These activities may be as simple as managing medications or paying bills.

The most well-known form is Alzheimer's type dementia. This type of dementia occurs in approximately 50% of patients with dementia. It is difficult to distinguish it clinically from other types of dementia. On autopsy, though, the microscopic impressions of Alzheimer's type dementia show a very specific quality that can be observed.

The second most common type of dementia is a vascular type dementia that occurs as a result of strokes or hardening of the arteries. Plaque build-up in the blood vessels of the brain leads to decreased blood flow, resulting in damage to the brain and the clinical symptoms of dementia. There are many other types of dementia, but Alzheimer's dementia and vascular dementia are the most common.

How does one know if they or a friend or family member has dementia? It is a clinical diagnosis that requires a history of functioning, either documented on standardized neuropsychological testing or other clinical assessments or documented by the decline of functioning known to close friends or family members. The immediate and short-term memory of individuals living with dementia is more immediately affected in earlier stages of the disease. Late-stage dementia affects your long-term memory. This would include the ability to recognize familiar faces. Individuals with dementia can many times remember very clearly what they were doing 50 years ago but cannot remember if they had breakfast or not or whether they are taking any medications. Short-term and long-term memory are laid down in the brain very differently. A great deal of research is being done on what causes the different types of dementia, as well as potential treatments. Is there any way to prevent dementia? At this time, probably not. But, knowing what to do if you develop dementia or if a family member or friend develops dementia can be very helpful.

There are certain medications widely prescribed that can affect the progression of the illness, but these will not cure dementia. It is noted that individuals with certain types of dementia respond better with these types of medications in the earlier stages of the illness. Later stages of the illness appear to be less responsive to currently available medicines.

In later stages of the illness, a small percent of individuals might have some significant behavioral changes that might require antipsychotic medications or mood stabilizers. Geriatric psychiatry units are available to assess and treat individuals in different stages of dementia and with different mood disorders and behavioral reactions that occur as a result of the dementia.

A common mood disorder associated with dementia is depression. When patients start realizing that they are unable to do the things that they could do when they were younger, clinical depression may ensue. Support of close friends and family members is essential when depression occurs with dementia. It is also possible that some type of prescribed antidepressants could minimize the symptoms.

Taking care of an individual with dementia can be extremely exhausting. You may have great intentions to take care of your parents, friend, or spouse who develops dementia. Dementia can be a very long-term and debilitating process. No one person can take care of an individual with dementia. It takes a group of people either on a dementia unit in a nursing home setting or group of people in a home environment. There is a new trend across the United States and Canada for the development of what are called "greenhouses." These are places to live for individuals with dementia that provide a cheery and relaxing environment along with needed medical care. The layout of these greenhouses allow for family members to visit and participate in meals. Everyone has their individual room which opens up into a large gathering area for the meals and socialization. These greenhouses do not have the same stigma attached to hospitals and traditional nursing homes.

Whether it is just forgetting where your keys are, forgetting large blocks of life, or losing the ability to remember things or function in social settings, everyone will experience some level of forgetfulness. It is natural for individuals to want to be as independent as possible, but it is also important that, when individuals become a danger to themselves or other people, activities such as driving are curtailed.

Educate yourself as to the signs and symptoms of dementia so that you or a family member or friend can be better prepared to deal with what may lie ahead.

LICENSE TO KILL

In geriatric psychiatry, one of the most common topics that individuals and families confront in the aging process is elderly driving. With an aging population, more and more stories appear of tragedies involving seniors.

Losing one's ability to drive a car is a major loss of independence and changes many aspects of a senior's life. It is perhaps one of the things in life that we all fear and dread, not only because of what driving allows, but also as a marked change in our status. Just as earning our driver's license at 16 is a rite of passage toward becoming an adult, the loss of our license confirms that we are no longer able to do something we may have valued for decades.

While it would be nice to believe that all of us would realize when it is time to stop driving and let others help us maintain a new type of independence, that is often not the case. Sometimes, it takes a catastrophic motor vehicle accident to end one's driving career.

From a professional perspective, there is not a certain age that someone should not be able to drive. The test – as it is at any age – is the functional ability to drive. There are 18-year-olds who are impaired due to chemical dependency, emotional disorders, or perhaps a physical disorder that cannot drive. There are many 80-year-old individuals who drive well without any restrictions.

For individuals with advancing forgetfulness, it is important to be honest with our families, friends, and healthcare professionals so that an accurate assessment of our ability to drive can be made. If we drive past our ability to function as alert, competent, and conscientious drivers, we might harm, injure, or kill another individual. That is not just a tragedy for us; it can change the lives of many other people who face injury or death caused by us driving beyond our ability to do so safely. It can become a very painful and unrelenting memory that can crowd out many of the joyful thoughts of our later years.

Driving is a privilege. A driver's license is a privilege. The message is the same to all ages.

Do not drive when you are impaired for whatever reason.

This can include driving under the influence of alcohol or other drugs. This could include driving when excessively fatigued. This could include driving with dementia or other type of medical problem that impairs your ability to think clearly. Do not drive past a safe age and harm someone else.

It is important for families to have discussions about driving as this is also an end-of-life issue. It is important to have that conversation with treating healthcare professionals.

When it is time to surrender your driver's license, please do it.

Driving past the point where we can safely do so turns a driver's license into something very deadly – a license to kill.

TELLING TALES

Storytelling is an art. There is nothing like being around a great storyteller at a campfire, family dinner, or public presentation. The combination of words used – and not used – and the timing and flow of the story cannot just recount a memory but make a new one too. Add to that a great voice, and many people are enchanted.

Storytelling – or the oral tradition, as anthropologists and sociologists would call – is as old as human kind. More than just communicating facts, storytelling relays ideas, images, and feelings. Occasionally, even truths are passed on (this is rarely the case when the topic is fishing). It not only served as entertainment but was part of the bonding for a family, clan, and even culture. The best of these stories were told by the leaders, elders, bards, poets, and sometimes fools.

Each language has one or more words for storyteller. The French call their storytellers counteurs, the Scots are known as shennachie, the Germans are erzähler, Shuōshū rén in China, and sheha if you speak Swahili. Perhaps the Irish have the best reputation for the gift of the gab or blarney.

Most children begin their young lives with bedtime stories. Some of these are repetitive stories featuring similar characters that experience life in a similar way to the children hearing them. Other stories introduce far away places or different experiences well beyond their early experiences. Eventually, it is time for fairy tales that can include the fanciful, delightful, and often scary characters that inhabit those worlds. Children like things to be a little scary sometimes – especially when safe in their beds with mom or dad reading to them (though there is the still that concern about the monster under the bed and the creepy characters hiding in the closets).

An important opportunity for senior members of the clan is to pass along the stories of the family. These can be favorite anecdotes from the childhood or life of the teller or the listener. The stories begin to fill in for the younger family members what life was like before their time. It also reminds the family of the ups and downs of life. Listeners learn how the older family members celebrated and struggled with the opportunities and challenges that they faced. Funny stories remind the listeners that the unexpected does happen and suggest how to roll with the punches life offers.

Less obvious but more important in these stories are the values that they pass along. When life happens, what do you choose to do? How do you deal with disappointment? How do you make tough choices? What do you do with success when it happens? All these kinds of values are tucked within the stories. Taken together, you begin to see what matters in the life of this family or clan. These are the things that are universal, or they may be elements of life that we approach differently than others do. If your family is one of faith, some of the stories may be keys to interpreting how to make sense out of the seemingly random events in life.

Telling the family stories also by definition means that the characters in the story are worth remembering. That also becomes a value that is passed along. Each life is full of countless experiences. Some of these moments are remarkable, while many are just the routines of life. To recount them all would take a lifetime and more. What is selected for a story shines a spotlight on a person, place, and time worth noting.

Most families come equipped with one or more storytellers to keep the tales alive. If you are already one of those, keep it up – you matter to your family circle. If you are not the natural storyteller, you are not off the hook.

Your life is an accumulation of those stories you have heard along with those you have lived so far. These stories combined with your other family traditions, customs, and beliefs make up your heritage. A heritage continues to have some ongoing elements to it, but it is always changing with each generation as new people join the family through marriage and birth and as people move to different places. Even the variety of careers will change the family's story. This has become even truer over the recent centuries when people no longer lived where their forbearers did and did not necessarily continue the farming or labor of their ancestors.

If you are in the third act of your life, it is time to tell your stories. Get over the notion that there is nothing worthy of a story. To begin to identify stories to tell, here are some simple questions.

What events in your life were surprises? What funny moments happened to you or while you were watching? When were you afraid? What were the best moments of your life? Who were the interesting people you met? How is life different now from when you were younger? If you could go back in time, when would you aim for and why?

Questions trigger stories.

How do you shape your stories? All those lessons in elementary school were valuable after all. There is a beginning, middle, and end. There are characters and a setting for the story. Persons, places, and things all fit in with the time of the tale.

Great storytellers use words to paint pictures so that you believe that you are there. They start out with some facts and then pose the problem or set up the surprise. After that, you have the twist or terror that gets the listener's attention. Finally, you finish with the wrap-up of the story.

Storytelling is an art, and there are some people more gifted at doing it. Like many things in life, it is not just for the experts. Venture into the world of storytelling with children and grandchildren. Have some stories on hand that pass on what interested you in the lives of the grandparents, aunts, uncles, and friends who are now gone. Passing on the stories not only keeps their memories alive – it strengthens your family ties for the generations that follow.

LEAN ON ME

Dealing with a chronically or terminally ill spouse can be a strange mixture of frustration, fatigue, and unexpected joy. Many people make a promise in their youth to a spouse to remain with them "in sickness and in health." What most people think on during those wedding vows are the illnesses that come and go with time. They might even envision the idea of old age. It rarely crosses our mind that our spouse might actually develop a chronic or terminal illness.

What are the best ways to support and care for a chronically ill spouse who has more sickness than health?

Hillary Clinton made the phrase "It takes a village" popular through her book on the care and nurture of children. That idea is also a useful concept for those with a spouse with a long-term or terminal illness. No one person, no matter how well-intentioned or heroic or loving, can do it all. It takes a network.

The network of support is for not only that spouse who is ill, but also for the spouse who is caring for their loved one. Who is in the network will depend on the nature of the illness as well as the proximity and age of close family and friends, healthcare providers, clergy, and home and agency support as available. Depending on the needs of the spouse that is ill, there could be additional financial challenges, physical challenges, and emotional challenges to the couple.

The best solution is always to plan in advance so that you can be proactive rather than reactive. Proactive steps would include taking out necessary disability insurance and life insurance before it is actually needed. It is also important to have some savings set aside to pay for unforeseen health care costs and pharmacy bills.

At some point, the ill spouse may have increasing physical needs. Someone may be needed to help physically bathe, feed, and help move the ill spouse. Often, you may not be able to provide that assistance yourself and may need the physical help of someone else to do that with or for your spouse. That might be someone close, or it may require a professional service to do safely.

Review your long-term health care policy or benefits to understand the range of services that are already covered. If you are considering buying insurance, it is usually more affordable before such an illness occurs.

More and more people are finding enough support through community and government agencies to allow them the option of staying at home longer rather than moving to a residential care or nursing home facility. It may come to the point when the necessary care cannot be given at home, and then it is time to move your loved one into another place of care.

For those who are terminally ill, many communities offer specialized support through hospice programs that can assist the ill spouse, the caring spouse, and their families at home or in the hospital. Some hospice villages now offer a positive and caring residential place for the final stages of the journey for the patient and their families during that difficult time.

Do not minimize the significance of the emotional issues that occur when your spouse is chronically or terminally ill. Chronic illness is emotionally wearing on the person who is ill as well as their spouse, family members, and friends. It is very draining emotionally to give and give to a disabled spouse even when you are motivated out of a loving commitment to each other. Many times, dealing with a chronically or terminally ill spouse can lead to clinical depression and anxiety in the caring partner. It might be important to seek out professional counseling, guidance, or even psychiatric care if required on this difficult journey. There are support groups for individuals dealing with chronically ill spouses in the medium and large-sized cities of America and Canada. Knowing that you are not the only one dealing with a spouse who is so ill and receiving feedback from others can be very therapeutic and healing.

Caring for a terminally or chronically ill spouse is a marathon and not a sprint. You need to look at this as a long-term opportunity and challenge.

It is okay to be angry, it is okay to be in denial, it is okay to bargain with God, and it is also okay to accept that this is the situation. Many times, the chronically ill spouse and his or her partner go through the same stages of grief. Sometimes, the stages of the spouse who is ill might occur at a different time than yours if you are the caregiver. It is important to be aware of emotional issues as you care for a chronically ill spouse.

It is also okay to consider the opportunity to be part of a chronically ill spouse's life as a joy and pleasure. It can be very satisfying to care for someone who has been an important part of your story when they are in need.

But, it is also important to remember that we are not Superman or Superwoman. We cannot do this on our own. It takes a village. It takes a network. Seek and use the help of individuals for support and direct care and counseling for other unexpected challenges and needs. It is okay to ask people for help. Do not assume that everyone around you knows what is going on in your life. Do not assume that everyone around you knows what you and your chronically ill spouse need at the time.

Tell people what you need. You might be surprised at what happens. With today's social networking and email, it can be easier to convey personal and medical needs. Some individuals set up a blog or use websites dedicated to providing updates for the family and friends of one who is ill. Give regular and frequent health reports and needs reports so that family and friends can understand how your chronically ill spouse is doing and what they can do to help. Do not hesitate to pull out all the stops to receive help. Dealing with a chronically or terminally ill spouse can be overwhelming.

If you are the spouse of a partner with a chronic or terminal illness, you may have your own challenges in needing and accepting the support of your loved one. You may feel guilty because you are no longer able to do everything you used to do in your relationship. It becomes easy to see how much your spouse and family have to adapt to your illness. You may be tempted to be the hero and minimize the support that your illness requires to avoid being "a burden" on your loved ones. It may be that you are fearful or depressed by the life changes that the illness has brought.

That may trigger a grasping at those closest to you to be with you all the time and provide everything for you.

The spouse who is ill must allow others to express their love and devotion by being there for you and with you during your difficult time. Do not push them away. At the same time, understand that no one person can or should do it all. Encourage and welcome the network of family, friends, and healthcare support to allow your spouse and family to survive this long road that you all are on. Ensure that they take time to refresh and be refreshed, which is a sign of your love and devotion to them too.

Remember that it takes a village. It takes a network.

Lean on me, but do not lean on me alone.

EMPTY CHAIRS AND EMPTY TABLES

Everyone born is on temporary assignment. We learn early on that not everyone who is in our life today will be there tomorrow. Often, it is a great-grandparent or grandparent who first passes from our everyday life into memory. Tragically, some who should not die at their age and stage of life also are gone. To live is to say goodbye as well as hello.

By the time you reach the third act of your life, many who would have shared your story are gone. The passing of the elderly is processed when we are small by our questions of death and what's next. We pause as we hear parents and others refer to a death as tragic because the one who passed was so young. What "young" means depends on the person who is speaking. They may have been referring to their contemporaries who were then in their 50s or 60s. Great shock and sadness are felt whenever a young person dies or one has a young family left behind. Heartbreak spreads whenever a child dies, no matter what the cause.

As we age, the ancient, elderly, and declining members of the fifth and sixth decade of life start to look younger and younger. Before long, we are in those decades with a renewed awareness that not everyone will make it to this decade as we did. Even people who are ten or fifteen years our senior are not that old. We soon are invited to join the AARP in the United States or the CARP in Canada. Special menus with senior discounts at restaurants and other bargains for those 55 and up can be disconcerting or rewarding depending on how you feel about getting older.

Knowing as we gather around our family table that people no longer are present where they once were can bring sadness. The grieving process can be most acute at those times and in those places where someone now gone was always present. The special occasions like Mother's and Father's Day, along with Thanksgiving, Christmas, or birthdays, can be especially difficult even many years later. The very rituals that create celebration and memories can become bittersweet as we note who is no longer there to join in the laughter and the stories.

It is a good reminder to tell their stories and remind others of the life they lived. Each of these people is a thread in the tapestry of your life and, by extension, of the lives that you touch. Family history also helps individuals to have a context for understanding who we are. Thinking outside the present is also a reminder that we are children of our time and that it is helpful to take a larger perspective on life. This perspective guards against the kind of unhealthy self-interest that can consume a generation that thinks the universe starts and stops with itself. Telling one's story also helps as a comfort to the storyteller. When you experience a loss, one of the ways that grief does its work is as you remember that person and talk about the things that you valued.

The empty chairs and empty tables serve as a reminder for us to pay attention to the people in our lives today. There is no guarantee that any of them will be around tomorrow – as unlikely as that might seem. Invest the time to be with them. Tell them how much you appreciate them. Share with them the favorite stories about them that make them special to you. For those you love – tell them that you love them.

Life is not long enough for anyone to do everything that they might do. Be sure that you use the years that you have been given to connect with the people in your story. Then, when it comes time to see an empty chair at their place, you will know that your relationship was solid and that they knew how important they were to you. That will make the empty chairs and empty tables a little easier to see.

THE REST IS HISTORY

Generations shape each other. One generation, through the struggles and successes it knows, creates in the next generation opportunities and reactions that influence how they see themselves and their world. For many centuries, this was a very local experience. The local village was home for generations. The way of life was handed down and largely adopted. As the opportunity to leave the rural life for the city developed, it was a much larger group of the older generation that would impact the younger. Emigration to other countries to avoid famine or find better opportunities changed that scale again.

Mass media in the late 19th and early 20th centuries in the form of newspapers, magazines, and books began the sense of generational thought being identified and described in ideas, advertising, music, and movements across borders. Radio, movies, and the mass-publication of magazines and books, followed by television, accelerated this. Voices of a generation could be heard distinctly from each other. Generations developed a gap.

Now that we live in a fast-flowing tide of information that circles the world instantly, generational shifts can be identified and quantified quickly. Social trends that once took many generations to develop can now move in a decade.

With all the benefits of this rapid change, it is increasingly difficult for a generation to pause and have a sense of "other" too. Apart from watching a period drama, visiting a museum, or seeing an old movie, it is difficult to personally connect with the past.

Families have the opportunity to do this through storytelling, memorabilia, and passing along the traditions. What can you do to help the coming generations have a sense of history and place?

There are many ways to do this. Think about which solutions fit you and your family the best. Here are some possibilities.

Organize your story.

Just as you would expect in a television interview, think of questions someone in the future watching highlights of your story would pose. Include biographical questions: where you were born, parents, siblings, grandparents, where you lived, members of your family, where you went to school, career, sports you played, and so on.

Take it a step deeper by talking about things you liked to do. What were the happiest moments in your life? Who were your best friends? What were the tough times? What did you imagine life would be like when you were young? How did that change as you lived your life? What are some of the most important things you learned about life? Think of things you wished you knew about your parents, grandparents, and beyond.

Who were the people who made your life better? Talk about family members, teachers, coaches, friends, and others who added to your wonderful life. Describe how they were a positive influence in your experience. If you have not told these people how they have blessed you and you still can – do it!

Connect the generations through your stories. You have memories of great-grandparents, grandparents, and others who were gone before the next generation met them. Describe what they were like. Tell stories about knowing them. Your stories are a living link to these other people who may now only appear in old photos or on a family tree. Your memories will keep their memories alive.

What were your greatest achievements? As you think about this, it may occur to you that some of the great items from a resume are not ultimately what you end up valuing the most. Explore what was most important in retrospect. That might be a very different set of experiences that will affirm to others what you truly valued. Sometimes, the greatest contributions we make are not ones we knew at the time would be most valuable.

Arrange an interview.

Have a relative with a video camera (they are everywhere!) meet you for an interview. Find a comfortable spot indoors or out. Give them the questions in advance. Record the interview. Unless they are someone who likes to edit, just keep the interview unedited – warts and all. Many people have stories sitting on a tape or hard drive that never reappear because they are waiting for someone to edit them. Tell the person doing the video that you just want them to record it and give it to you in a format that you can share as you wish. You are much more likely to get a volunteer to do the recording, and it is much more likely to be seen that way. Do not be too ambitious for each session. Start with the idea of an hour and keep it to that. Depending on how comfortable you are in sharing your stories, that might be enough or just the beginning. The process can be tiring, so do not try to do a marathon (your camera person will thank you).

Write some stories.

If you are more comfortable writing than speaking, write down your tales. You do not have to imagine a full autobiography – that will usually keep you from ever starting anything. Instead, write down a "blog-sized" article about one aspect of your life. Do a page about something from your story.

Organize the photo albums.

Gather the many pictures and papers in your history to start a photo album or scrap book. Remember to add dates and names of people where you can.

Will your history.

Rather than just leave everything in your estate to be sorted out by others after you are gone, take the time to identify particular pieces of jewelry, family heirlooms, and other keepsakes to specific people. Include with those gifts the story of the item so that this too could be passed along to future generations. Identify the people associated with it and why it was special. Some people do a video recording that shows the items and tells the stories. That will give those receiving the items a sense of connection that goes deeper than whatever the item appears to have on its own. It also creates a sense of it being entrusted to them to perhaps pass along to another generation as well.

Life is lived. History is recorded. Do your part to share your story for those who wish they knew more about you and your life.

THE LAST STOP

It is best to deal with end-of-life decisions sooner than later. If these decisions are not made ourselves, someone else will make them for us. In some cases, it will be other family members or perhaps the government. This adds an extra burden for those who love and care for you during a difficult time.

What kind of questions and decisions need to be answered before the end of life?

Regarding end-of-life health decisions, it is important to have a living will. A living will is a legal document that you set up to let family members, physicians and friends know how aggressive you want medical treatment to be at the end of your life. Many times, these decisions are specific with quality-of-life issues. For instance, if someone has had widespread cancer and there is no chance of recovery, it might be that she would choose a DNR (or do-not-resuscitate) status. This instructs health care providers, family, and friends that if you quit breathing or your heart stops, no heroic efforts will be made to prolong misery. There are also those who want family, physicians, and friends to be as aggressive as possible, no matter what the situation.

Another option for facing end-of-life medical decisions is hospice care. Hospice care is a very compassionate, kind way of dealing with end of life with dignity and respect. Hospice care provides palliative care such as pain medications and other medical measures to keep the patient comfortable. Hospice care can be delivered in the home, in the hospital, or at a growing number of dedicated hospice care facilities. No heroic medical interventions occur during hospice care treatment. At times, patients get better in hospice care and are removed from hospice care, but generally, that is not the case.

Your wishes regarding a funeral can also be very helpful for your family to know. Pre-planning your funeral ensures that those who are wishing to honor your memory as they grieve their loss of you will have the added comfort that they knew what you wanted.

Other important things to consider towards the end of life are having a will. All adults should have a written will. Without this, your wishes may not be known, and there may be delays and additional costs to your estate for the government to process what you leave behind to those people and causes that you care about. Sadly, the lack of a will can lead to many painful experiences for those left behind. Legal battles between competing parties can last for years after you are gone. Conversely, when there is a clearly drawn will in place, everyone knows clearly your wishes. Consult your attorney to ensure you have thought about all the contingencies that might not be obvious to people trying to create their own wills.

If an individual becomes demented or in other ways mentally incapacitated, a family member, friend, or other entity will need to take over conservatorship or guardianship of health care decisions and decisions regarding the will and handling finances. Again, it is better to have determined these earlier in life than when it is too late. If you wait until it is too late, individuals who may not have your best interests in mind will be making those decisions for you.

Many people put off these sometimes uncomfortable topics, always assuming that there will be time. As many families learn, illness and death do not always wait for us to have everything in order.

Have courage and make your wishes known.

THE GREY HAVENS

At the end of the epic Lord of the Rings trilogy by J. R. R. Tolkien, many of the principal characters were at a port known as The Grey Havens to say goodbye.

Some would be returning to their homelands now that the forces of evil in their time had been defeated. Hobbits would return to Hobbiton, and men would return to their cities. A few were about to take a voyage across the sea to a very different place. They were about to leave Middle Earth to go to Valinor, the Undying Lands – home of the Valar and original home of the elves. Many elves had already left Middle Earth for the journey back. In this scene with the great white ship waiting in the background, it was Gandalf the wizard and the great elves Lord Elrond and Lady Galadriel who were waiting to take the journey. Joining them would be two of the ring bearers, Bilbo Baggins and his nephew, Frodo.

What were the Undying Lands like? In a dark moment where both were facing death in the battle for Gondor at Minas Tirith, Gandalf spoke of it to the young hobbit Pippin in the movie version.

PIPPIN: I didn't think it would end this way.

GANDALF: End? No, the journey doesn't end here. Death is just another path, one that we all must take. The grey rain-curtain of this world rolls back, and all turns to silver glass, and then you see it.

PIPPIN: What? Gandalf? See what?

GANDALF: White shores, and beyond, a far green country under a swift sunrise.

PIPPIN: Well, that isn't so bad.

GANDALF: No. No, it isn't.

Gandalf was returning to the place that was his home before being sent on this mission to serve Middle Earth. He had departed Valinor some two thousand years earlier.

For human beings, what follows death is one of the "known unknowns" in life. There are many views of what happens after death ranging from nothingness to becoming part of the cosmic energy to reincarnation or some form of afterlife in heaven, hell, or something in between, like purgatory, with many other variations in between.

Like our understanding of life, some of these questions of philosophy and theology impact many of the choices we make along the way. A person who views life as a random series of events interprets their experiences in a different way than someone who believes in a general Providence or that God is purposefully engaged in our lives. While this book is not intended to be a book on life after death, understanding how your view will impact your life choices is a part of finishing well.

It is true to say that there are some people who believe that there is no consciousness after death who finish well. It is also true that not everyone who believes in God's providence has a happy ending.

We do believe that there is more to life than the physical world we know through our five senses. The gap between our senses and this belief in a God who is revealed and who chooses to participate in our lives is correctly called faith. For us, God's presence on our life journey does not mean that we will be immune to the trials and tribulations of the human experience. Nor do we believe that this means that we will not fail in our life choices too. But, on the journey and through the good and bad choices that make up every human story, our lives are part of something more. We do believe that each and every human being has dignity and value as part of God's universe. We are also purposed to serve others along the way with the gifts, talents, opportunities, and time we have been given here. This affects our first, second, and third acts.

Heaven, in our Christian view, is not the destination we earn but the gift we are given. It is the Undying Land free from the limitations, sickness, suffering, and death that we know in this life.

We share Tolkien's view that death is not the end but just another path that we all must take. That helps people to be free to live this life with its wonder and challenges to the full knowing that it is only the beginning of the story. For us, it gives us a hopeful strength as we approach the difficulties of the third act.

THE MUSIC BOX

An old and enchanting sound in many homes is a music box. Long before our age where any type of music can be heard anywhere and played at any time on the myriad of devices we now enjoy, it often was a music box that filled a room with song.

Perhaps you heard one as a child that played Brahms's Lullaby that might have helped you fall asleep. As you grew up, you might be trusted to hold the box as it played. Eventually, you could turn the key on the bottom to wind up the box so that the music might play again. As you opened the lid, a ballerina or other character might dance or move. Some boxes allowed you to see the cylinder turn with the small bumps lifting and then releasing the fine metal teeth that created the sound.

Like many special items, music boxes have their own personality. Choices of design and especially song gave each box a unique character and appeal. The music box became a special gift to give or receive at important life milestones as a romantic gift or to mark something new like the arrival of a baby.

Their presence at that younger age of our life, along with the emotional connection, often made the music box a favorite item to touch and play with when visiting our parents' home later in life. For many, the music box became an item to cherish as it was passed down through generations.

The song that the music box played was always the same one. We soon learned the melody, and we could anticipate each note. If the music was associated with lyrics, we might sing along with the tune.

If you remember your music box, you might recall how the sound of the tune would change as the box wound down. The beginning – when the spring on the mechanism was tight –meant that the song was lively and quick. The notes seemed to blur over each other as the song sped along its course. Humming or singing along, we would have to hurry to keep up with the fast pace. Gradually and almost imperceptibly, the cadence would slow down until the tune was playing at a rate that was more familiar. The cylinder was still plucking the same tines as before, but the song now seemed graceful and even. Eventually, the song would slow down to a more elegant and gentle tempo where each note became clearer. The final part of the journey slowed to the point that each note was distinct and would hang in the air before it shared time and space with the next until ultimately the song stopped.

Life's song has a similar pattern if we live long enough to experience the changes and gain the perspective that age and experience brings. The rush of our youth, with the high energy and invincibility of that stage, is like the beginning of the song of the music box. We hear the song, but the notes are blurred by the high tempo and strength of that fully wound spring released to announce it is alive. As with all the stages of human development, this is as it should be.

Before long, we have grown up, completed education, entered relationships, and begun our work in the blur that is the beginning of adulthood. So many great and momentous decisions are made. They open and close doors that will never again be so easy to pass through or perhaps even find. Little wonder that so much is said about the folly of youth.

But how can we blame the young for reacting so to the choices that society presents them with? Time and money are often cited as the two commodities that often do not align together – when we have the time to do things, we often do not have the money and vice versa. Perhaps we should also contrast youth and retirement since our retirement would be a very different experience if you had all the advantages of health and energy that our early years provided. Would you have preferred to enjoy retirement until you were 30, then start your career and work an extra ten years on the other end? That would be a very different retirement. But would it be a better one?

As we settle into the demanding decades of the 30s and 40s, we begin to develop a confidence that is not based on our energy alone. We add experience to our quiver, and that allows us to see opportunities and dangers with a different perspective. Like the slowing song of the music box, we begin to move to the music confidently with a new-found grace and rhythm that can be sustained. The building decades of the 30s and 40s require our ability to join the dance and keep moving with it.

The song slows again as we enter our 50s and 60s, where we find the beginnings of wisdom. At last, we begin to understand the song that has been playing all along. We hear in a new way that familiar melody that no longer requires us to think about the moves of the dance but that is now part of us. Our life often now begins to appear make sense as we see the threads that connect our early experiences with who we have become. We begin to accept ourselves for who we are and what we have become even though that can be very different from the person of the early verses of our song. Many of the worries that would panic us in our youth give way to the confidence of experience. You have survived so many of the challenges of life that might have been unthinkable a few decades earlier. There are new questions about life that would not have occurred to you in years gone by. You begin to recognize that there may be more time behind you than ahead. What does my life mean?

How quickly the song slows again depends in part with how your music box was wound at the beginning. Some songs continue to play on with a strong tempo for a decade or two more. Others begin to hear the call of three-score and ten as normal life. Beyond 70, we feel that we are on borrowed time, knowing that many have not made it that far on the journey. We hear the tempo relax further, and for the first time, we begin to hear each of the notes in our song. If asked, we would have said long ago that our song had many individual notes in the composition. We could sing the song. But as each note plays with a pause in between, for the first time, we consider the role that each one has played in our song.

In our life, we begin to think about the people, places, and experiences that have made up our song. We can now begin to reflect on them in isolation and begin to realize how they gave our song shape. Some notes are sharp or flat. Some are held for a long time, others only for a quick moment. Familiar notes play over and over in our song, and other notes are heard only once. This is not much different than our family, friends, colleagues, and acquaintances. We can all think of key people who have journeyed along with us from beginning to end. We can think of others who were there for a part of the tale but who did not continue on for any of a thousand reasons. Many have enriched our life. Sadly, some caused us great pain. Much of this can not be truly sorted out and understood until we have the perspective of time and age.

Take a moment to listen to your life song.

What do you hear?

What does it mean to you?

A PRAYER FOR THE AGES

This prayer associated with St. Francis of Assisi captures the frustrations and aspirations of all of the stages of our lives. It has a renewed meaning when applied to those facing retirement and the changes that aging brings.

If you have not read it for a while, read it again and you might find it has a renewed application to your life as it is now.

Lord, make me an instrument of Your peace;
Where there is hatred, let me sow love;
Where there is injury, pardon;
Where there is error, truth;
Where there is doubt, faith;
Where there is despair, hope;
Where there is darkness, light;
And where there is sadness, joy.

O Divine Master, Grant that I may not so much seek
To be consoled as to console;
To be understood as to understand;
To be loved as to love.
For it is in giving that we receive;
It is in pardoning that we are pardoned;
And it is in dying that we are born to eternal life.

SECOND WIND

Races come in two varieties – sprints and marathons. Sprinters bursts out of the blocks and go full speed with whatever explosive energy they have. They give it their all right away to finish that shorter distance in what seems like a blur of arms and legs.

Marathons are a different type of race. The mental and emotional preparation is entirely other. This longer race is rarely about bursting out of the blocks and gaining and keeping a lead, full speed ahead. The marathon runner knows that they have to pace themselves to keep enough energy to finish well. This means a strong start followed by a careful pace. Depending on the length of the race, they may have to use a variety of strategies – including giving up, then retaking the lead – over the course of the contest. Their pace has to take into account the other competitors. If they try to keep up with the early leaders who are running at an unsustainable pace, they too will flare out before the race is half done. What a marathon runner trains for is to be winning at the end. One of the ingredients that can help them do this is what is called the second wind.

If you participate in sports – or remember doing so – you have experienced this magical power. Just as the initial burst of energy seems to be fading and you feel like you will not be able to continue, suddenly, the second wind arrives. Different than the initial strength and intensity of the sprint, the second wind is a sustaining energy where you do not feel the pain or fatigue you did but instead find yourself carried forward. It is a very strange experience but one that can be relied upon by athletes because it is always waiting for them if they can go far enough and long enough to find it.

Baby boomers that reach their 50s and beyond may come to feel that they too are a spent force. The pressures of building a career, paying mortgages, raising children, caring for aging parents, hints of chronic health issues, and a weariness of life can make you feel like you are ready to drop. The finish line seems a very long way down the track. It may feel like you will never get there. You might also wonder whether you want to get there if this is what it will feel like.

The good news is that there is a second wind awaiting those who persist into their fifties and beyond. So many of the worries and stresses begin to either recede or at least seem more manageable. The many life experiences and difficulties that you survived before now give you a confidence to face the challenges currently on your plate.

Another part of the second wind is a perspective on life. You begin to understand that what is important are the relationships and experiences that you have and continue to add to your story. A lifetime of accumulating things no longer satisfies. A renewed sense of who you are and what really matters starts to emerge for most people. You now seek contentment rather than achievement. The years of grasping and climbing give way to a renewed ability to see life as it is and what it might be. You begin to look backward at the generations who will follow. You now appreciate anew those generations who went before you and what gave their lives significance. Life gives you a second wind to have a second chance at the years that remain.

The second wind also gives you a new hope for your future. Life's disappointments and failures fade into the background as a sense of meaning and purpose emerges to give you a reason to keep on running. We finally begin to understand that we cannot change the past and that many things in our present and future cannot be controlled. Relaxing our grip allows us to begin to enjoy what has long been around us but that we missed due to our efforts to manage everything.

If you speak to many retirees, you hear them describe how they are busier now than ever they were. They wonder how they fit life in just a few years earlier. The lagging and stressed self of the fifties has given way to a positive and optimistic view of the time that remains.

The race still requires our participation to finish well. We do not meet our second wind and sit down. The gift of the second wind in our lives is to give us the possibility of making the most of those years left when boundless youthful energy and middle-age grit are spent. Life begins to have a more effortless quality to it and brings with it a confidence that allows us to face the challenges of the third act of our lives.

So, if you are pumping hard and feeling like the race cannot be finished, do not give up. Your second wind is not far away.

THE CURTAIN RISES
ONCE AGAIN

As we come to the end of this book, we would like to encourage you. The curtain may still be down if you have not yet started the third act of your life. Perhaps you are already retired and the curtain went up a while ago.

If you are entering or living in the third act, it is a time of great possibilities. You can make choices each day that will enhance the lives of those in your family, your friends, and your community. You have the power to be a positive part of the story of other people who may be celebrating life or who may be experiencing their own life challenges.

Some of the topics of aging are not easy. The golden years are not for the faint of heart. Then again, you probably did not get this far by taking the easy way out. A life well-lived seems destined to have its share of ups and downs, whether by our own making or though what life brings our way.

Each day we are given allows us to add new pages to our story. None of us knows how many pages and chapters remain. What will you do with the time that you have left?

Set aside those failures and hurts that slow you down. Break the chains of bitterness by forgiving others. Leave the "might have beens" and the would have, could have, should have, roads-not-taken questions for the critics to review later.

Gather together your many experiences, your talents, and your gifts. Combine them in the courage that you have learned resides deep within yourself. Then, find the people and opportunities that need someone just like you.

Choose to live the rest of your life with a sense of purpose and energy that comes from the wise urgency that age brings, knowing that time passes by so quickly.

Make the call, write the note, send the invitation, and connect with those who are available in your life. Spend time with the people who have been part of your story so far. Find some new ones to add to enrich your days ahead. Be an encourager.

What will your third act look and sound like? As you are its main character, expect to hear echoes of the first two acts. Themes begun and developed in your story will continue. While some of the lines that remain may already be written for you, expect the opportunity to improvise in your story. Put your head, your heart, and your hope into this performance that is your lifetime.

Too soon, the curtain falls on the lives of those we know and love. How they lived continues in our memories, shaping us as they did and do. Those remembered best often were those who had a memorable third act.

When your part in the great drama of human life is done, may you be remembered as one of those who finished well.

May your third act be your greatest yet!

END NOTES

As the writers of this book, we see ourselves less as authors and more as messengers who are passing along what we have received. We are indebted to many professors, teachers, mentors, authors, speakers, friends, and patients who have taught us about the topics considered in this book. There are too many sources to begin to credit – even if we could retrace where we first learned each underlying principle, concept, or perspective. The purpose here was to provide an accessible overview to allow the reader to think about his or her journey rather than to present an academic review of studies and data. As such, we include some end notes to highlight places for the reader to explore further on his or her own. We do not doubt that if we had the benefit of speaking with each of those who will read this book, we would have many additional ideas and perspectives to share.

Chapter

Creating Your Business Card

Dellinger, Susan. (1989). Psycho-geometrics: How to Use Geometric Psychology to Influence People. NJ: Prentice Hall.

Generation Next

There are many texts and courses in social psychology that deal with Erik Erikson's important contributions.

Erikson, E.H. (1968). Identity: Youth and Crisis. New York: Norton.

Erikson, E.H. (1963). Childhood and Society. (2nd ed.). New York: Norton.

Carver, C.S. & Scheir, M.F. (2000). Perspectives on Personality. Needham Heights, MA: Allyn & Bacon.

State Occasions

Kübler-Ross, Elisabeth. (1969). On Death and Dying. New York: Macmillan

Good Morning, Good Morning!

"A Crack In Time" was an ABC News presentation produced in 1978 that reviewed the many dramatic changes that occurred in social, political, and international relations. Like 9/11, it was one of those moments that seemed to mark a change in how life was viewed before and after.

Profits and Losses

See Generation Next references.

The Greatest Generation

Brokaw, Tom (1998). The Greatest Generation. New York: Random House.

Scrooge and Sawyer

Dickens, Charles. (1998) A Christmas Carol. New York: Putnam.

Twain, Mark. (1999) The Adventures of Tom Sawyer. Irving: Saddleback Educational

Predicting the Weather

Lewis, C. S. (2001)The Problem of Pain. New York: HarperOne.

Good Will

For more about financial, estate, and retirement planning, take a look at one of Grant's other books co-authored with Michael H. Lanthier.

Fairley, Grant D. & Lanthier, Michael H, (2013). Own Your Future – Wisdom for Wealth and a Better Tomorrow. Toronto: Silverwoods Publishing.

License to Kill

With smart cars that drive themselves in the not too distant future, driver's licenses may have new restrictions that reflect our cognitive challenges just as we currently require glasses or contacts for a person with limited vision. These experimental smart cars can already transport people who are blind. Persons with some cognitive challenges that would currently disqualify them from driving could also be able to use this new class of automobiles. Perhaps they would be limited to the "auto-pilot" mode vs. being able to take full control of the vehicle. That would allow for greater independence for a longer period of time for those who should not be driving any longer on their own.

The Grey Havens

The Return of the King. (2003). New Line Cinema.

A Prayer for the Ages

The prayer is popularly associated with St. Francis of Assisi, although it may have been written by someone in France in the early 1900s. We think the sentiment and message is worth repeating regardless of who created it.

http://en.wikipedia.org/wiki/Make_Me_an_Instrument_of_Your_Peace

RESOURCES

Personal and Professional Development

Strategic Seminars - Workshops and seminars for corporations and groups covering topics on business, leadership, motivation, relationships, team building, customer service, and more. There is a special focus on leadership and group development consulting for corporations. Seminars are offered in the U.S., Canada, and the Caribbean.
www.strategic-seminars.com

Canadian Executive Coaching - Executive coaching for Canadian senior executives, managers, department heads, top salespeople, and leaders. Serving a wide range of industry, government, and not-for-profit entities, Canadian Executive Coaching offers one-on-one coaching that improves performance, provides personal support, and facilitates reflection. Based on a whole-person model that recognizes your different skills, passions and abilities, Canadian Executive Coaching will help you reach your full potential as a leader and as a person.

This coaching service is now available worldwide online.
www.canadian-executive-coaching.com

Psycho-Geometrics® was formulated by Dr. Susan Dellinger, who used her skills as a communications specialist to design an incredibly intuitive yet accurate tool. It instantly identifies our communication style. The insight she had was to use the most common shapes of a circle, triangle, box, rectangle, and squiggly line. Once identified, she created very helpful descriptions that people usually find affirm their gut decision. As with a cool magic trick, you will want to know how she did it. This is one of the best ways to explore your communication styles that are so important to effectiveness in business and in life relationships. If you have never heard Susan speak, read the book, or taken the Psycho-Geometrics® test, you are in for a great "a-ha!" moment. Take the online or print Psycho-Geometrics® test. Enter the discount code "Wheaton" and receive a discount. **www.psychogeometrics.com**

U.S. Resources

National Council on Aging
www.ncoa.org

National Alliance on Mental Illness
www.nami.org

Alzheimer's Association
www.alz.org

National Institute on Aging
www.nia.nhi.gov

American Association of Retired Persons
www.aarp.org

Canadian Resources

Canadian Association of Retired Persons
www.carp.ca

Alzheimer Society of Canada
www.alzheimer.ca

Everything Zoomer
www.everythingzoomer.com

Canadian Mental Health Association
www.cmha.ca

National Seniors Council
www.seniorscouncil.gc.ca

Blair Lamb, M.D. – The Lamb Clinic has a special focus on fibromyalgia, migraines, arthritis, whiplash, and more. Extensive articles are included on a range of pain topics.
www.drlamb.com

Larry Komer, M.D. – information for women, covering such topics as menopause, bio-identical hormone therapies, breast cancer, and more. For men, you can learn about andropause, testosterone, fitness, and the various conditions affecting men. New understanding on traumatic brain injury is part of his research as well.

www.drkomer.com

www.mastersmensclinic.com

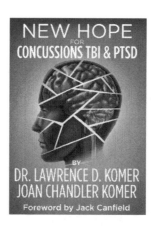

Dr. Larry Komer and **Joan Chandler Komer** offer new hope to those with injuries and their loved ones. This is a guide to explore what concussions, TBI and PTSD are. The book will be helpful for the injured person, their family, and for healthcare professionals. Dr. Komer shares his insights from the successful treatment of many patients at The Komer Brain Institute. Self-esteem coach, and educator Joan Chandler adds her valuable perspectives on how to cope with disappointments and loss often associated with injuries. Together, they share a powerful message of hope for the treatment of concussions, TBI, and PTSD.

A WHEATON MOMENT

Some people enjoy a very positive experience in their university life. Others come to appreciate it more once they have moved on with career and life. Those who enjoyed college life at the time and years later can look back on it fondly and have reason to be grateful.

For the authors in the late 1970s, Wheaton College, that small liberal arts Christian college west of Chicago, was such a place. Founded in 1860, the academically rigorous college also taught an integration of faith and learning that included attention to our development as whole persons. A Wheaton education included a call to serve others with whatever gifts, talents, and opportunities each was given.

Each class year consisted of only four hundred students from most of the 50 United States and many countries around the world. Experiencing community life as a residential college that included attention to our spiritual development gave us a valuable foundation for the years that would follow.

Led at the time by President Hudson Armerding, we were enriched by many wonderful professors who challenged and encouraged us. Like most alumni of any school, we look back on our years at the college as the best of times for us and for the institution.

We are grateful for the preparation Wheaton College gave us for our careers and life.

SILVERWOODS PUBLISHING

Executive coach and seminar speaker Grant D. Fairley takes you through the big ideas of leadership that he shares with leaders in seminars and during their professional development sessions. Whether you are leading in a corporation, government department, educational institution or community group, this book is for you. Develop your understanding of who you are, how to communicate effectively, ways to solve conflicts, and how to find satisfaction as a leader.

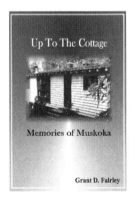

Silverwoods Publishing is the publisher of the book *Up to the Cottage - Memories of Muskoka,* which describes the joys and memories of simple cottages in the golden era of Muskoka. Grant D. Fairley recalls the heartwarming stories typical of life at cottages in the second half of the 20th Century. Whether you spent time in Muskoka, Haliburton, the Kawarthas or another place where cottages and cabins were your home away from home, this book is for you.

www.silverwoods-publishing.com

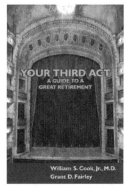

If life is a play with three acts in it, what will your third act be like?

Retirement triggers many changes in our life and prompts new questions.

What will mean to be retired? What do I have to do to be ready? How will my life be different? What are the risks and rewards of this stage of my journey? Will these by my golden years? How will my relationships change?

If you are already retired, what can you do to make this the most satisfying time of your life?

This book includes topics on: Family - Retirement – Purpose – Health – Friendships - Anti-aging – Meaning – Grief - Relationships – Brain Health - Legacy.

Discover the choices you can make to have a great retirement.

This book was originally written in 1928. The tale is told with the care of a historian and a minister's love of story. Reverend Hugh Cowan transports his readers back to pioneer life in this wonderful and wild part of Canada at an important time in our history. Cowan grew up in the Manitoulin Island and La Cloche areas of Georgian Bay. He returned to it many times over his life with some of his family remaining on the island and in the region to this day.

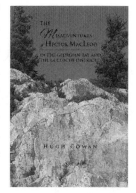

In 1937, minister and historian Rev. Hugh Cowan reflects at the end of four decades of ministry on the some of the big ideas of the Christian faith. He recounts some of the changes he has observed in Christian thought in the first half of the 20th Century. In this book, Cowan explores the realities of life and death as experienced with his congregations. Many of the challenges he discusses are just as relevant today.

"This world's a stage, a poet once sung, and on it each man must act his part. Another poet has said, "Change and decay in all around I see."

Two poets, one sees in human life a great drama, and every member of the human family performing a part in that drama; the other sees in human life, change and death.

In the great drama of human life, the producer of the drama is God; the Lord Jesus supplies to the stage its light; while the Spirit of God is the One who trains and disciplines and practises the actors so that each may do their part wisely and well, even perfectly. The members of the human family, the actors on the stage, some do their part wisely and well, never perfectly; some do their part not so wisely and not so well; others do not do their part at all; while still others are out in rebellion to destroy the good influence and effect of the drama, if they can."

This book is for everyone who wants to own their future. In a world where change is now normal, learn how to make career and financial decisions to build a better tomorrow for yourself and the ones you love. Whatever your age or stage in life, Fairley and Lanthier will show you how to have the courage to face your future with optimism and confidence.

Discover Your Oasis
Hope for Weary Caregivers
William S. Cook, Jr., M.D.
Grant D. Fairley

Psychiatrist William S. Cook, Jr., M.D. and executive coach Grant Fairley guide caregivers on how to find hope, refreshment, and satisfaction in their demanding careers. Compassion fatigue is an ever-present challenge for those who are committed to caring for and serving others. It is a resource for social workers, healthcare professionals, educators, ministers, first-responders, government, and leaders. It will also encourage those who care for a spouse or family member.

ABOUT THE AUTHORS

DR. WILLIAM S. COOK, JR. is a native of Jackson, Mississippi. His friendship with the co-author started many years ago at Wheaton College where he majored in biology. He returned home to Jackson, Mississippi to complete his medical school training at the University of Mississippi Medical School. He completed a flexible internship at Framingham Union Hospital in Framingham, Massachusetts, focusing on internal medicine. While pursuing his aspiration of being a dermatologist, Dr. Cook completed a year of pathology residency training at the Mallory Institute of Pathology at Boston City Hospital in Boston, Massachusetts. He then completed a National Institute of Health fellowship in dermatology at the University of California in San Francisco. Still unclear of his final direction in medicine, Dr. Cook worked in emergency medicine in both California and Mississippi. He went back to school to complete his residency training in psychiatry at the University of Mississippi Medical Center in Jackson, Mississippi, where he served as chief resident during his senior year. He received the Jaquith Award for most outstanding resident his senior year.

Dr. Cook then completed a fellowship in Public Psychiatry at Columbia University in New York along with a fellowship specializing in sexuality at Bellevue Hospital (NYU School of Medicine) in New York. He has been a psychiatrist for the last 20 years with a current private outpatient practice in Jackson, Mississippi, along with working part time in Natchez, Mississippi. He currently lives in Jackson, Mississippi. Dr. Cook has had the opportunity to travel worldwide to over 60 countries. He is looking forward to going to the Congo to see the lowland gorillas within the next year.

Bill would like to dedicate this book to his partner, Jay Barrier, as they grow older together; his parents, who have provided him love, an education, and guidance over the years; Myrna Kruckeberg, a friend and mentor; Dr. Brenda Hines; and other professional colleagues, family, and friends who have enriched his life over the years.

Learn more about Bill on his website **www.williamscookjrmd.com. Follow Bill on Twitter @drwilliamscook**

Bill would welcome your comments on the book. You may contact him at cook@silverwoods-publishing.com

GRANT D. FAIRLEY is a principal speaker with Strategic Seminars, a division of McK Consulting Inc. His seminars cover a wide range of topics, including leadership, finance, team building, sales training, relationships, communication, conflict management, personal development, motivation, creativity, and more.

He serves as an executive coach providing professional development, support, and perspectives to senior executives in business, government, sales, and other organizations.

Grant is a graduate of Wheaton College, Wheaton, Illinois.

Over the years, he has had a liberal arts life with a range of activities that include teaching, writing, and encouraging as the common threads in the many roles.

Grant has written or co-authored a number of books that are published by Silverwoods Publishing.

In addition to writing books, he is the co-author of a number of patents relating to technology and healthcare.

Faith, family, and friends continue to be the essential ingredients in Grant's life from which he finds meaning and satisfaction each day.

Grant would like to thank Cari for her love, friendship, and support during the writing of this book. While she regularly accused him of being old before his time, she has kept him young in spite of his love of history, past-times, and old stories. Before they knew it, Grant and Cari became an old story too, but one that is still full of adventure.

He dedicates this book to the many older family members and friends of previous generations who have shown by example how to celebrate life while facing the challenges of aging.

Follow Grant on Twitter @grantfairley.

Grant would welcome your comments on the book. You may contact him at fairley@silverwoods-publishing.com

Silverwoods
Publishing

Manufactured by Amazon.ca
Bolton, ON